AF576635

AMERICAN NAVAL BROADSIDES

Old Ironsides on a Lee Shore

AMERICAN NAVAL BROADSIDES

A Collection of Early Naval Prints (1745-1815)

by Edgar Newbold Smith

Foreword by M. V. Brewington

Philadelphia Maritime Museum

and

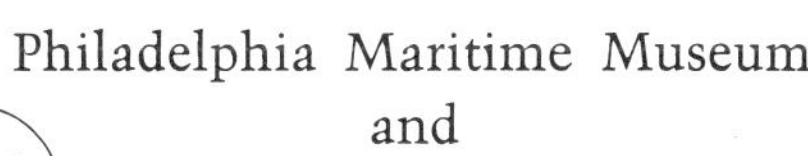

Clarkson N. Potter, Inc./Publisher

New York

Printed in the United States of America by Nimrod Press
Library of Congress Catalog Card Number: 74-83106
Published simultaneously in Canada by General Publishing Company Limited.
Inquiries should be addressed to
Clarkson N. Potter, Inc., 419 Park Avenue South, New York, N.Y. 10016.
First Edition

CONTENTS

To
Captain William Bispham Black, USMC, 1892-1918
killed in action at St. Mihiel
and
Colonel William Dulty Smith, USMC, 1883-1965

LIST OF ILLUSTRATIONS

FOREWORD

Since the end of the Second World War when the United States Navy emerged as the greatest sea power on earth, its history and chronology have been the subject of extensive study. Amateur and professional historians alike have dug into almost every known detail and have published extensively every imaginable phase. In the pictorial field, we have seen the publication of four attempts at a complete record of American naval prints and paintings, from simple listings of the pieces without comment to full dress reproductions of all the items in color or black and white, accompanied by the scholarly apparatus of bibliography and iconography. The majority of the resulting books have been private publications, available only to a few friends of the authors. Now, with the imprimatur of a distinguished marine museum, we have a catalog of a great collection of American naval prints, most of its holdings having been reproduced here in color, together with all the scholarship anyone could wish.

Beginning in the mid-eighteenth century with the attack on Louisburg, we depended for our art work largely on foreign-trained artists. This situation continued throughout the Revolutionary War; many of the major naval battles, such as the *Serapis-Bon Homme Richard* action, were rendered in paintings and engravings by Englishmen. The Conyngham raids on merchant shipping in the Channel and North Sea were depicted by Dutch artists. The Quasi-War actions were reported pictorially by Birch and Savage, both British-born and trained. The Barbary Wars introduced us to Mediterranean painters such as Cornè, Guerrazzi, Baugean and the Roux family. During the War of 1812, the now Americanized Thomas Birch and Cornè—plus a few venturesome native Americans such as Strickland and Abel Bowen—began to try their hands in competition with prints made abroad.

It is easy to determine the favorite actions in each war, favored sometimes for inconsistent reasons. During the Revolution, the *Bon Homme Richard-Serapis* engagement is far and away first with both the British and the Americans. In fact, sixteen prints are known, plus an unrecorded number of original oils, watercolors and drawings. No other episode of the war inspired as many works, partly because of its controversial outcome. The British did their best to claim the action a victory for the Royal Navy because the *Serapis* had enabled the Baltic Convoy to escape untouched; the Americans claimed a victory because the *Serapis* surrendered.

During the War of 1812 the favorite action was between the *Constitu-*

tion and the *Guerriere,* with thirty-one prints and innumerable originals. In this engagement there was nothing for the British to cheer about, and the Americans had everything; the enemy ship was sent to the bottom, the American crew had a small casualty list, and the *Constitution* was scarcely damaged.

Tied with the *Constitution-Guerriere* prints in American popularity during this period was the *United States-Macedonian* action. This time the British vessel was captured, brought into a safe harbor and eventually became a regularly commissioned ship in the United States Navy. Also notable during the War of 1812 were the prints of the Battle of Lake Erie, which resulted in not only an American victory but a quotable phrase as well: "We have met the enemy and they are ours."

Almost the equal of any of these prints was one of an action in which we could take no pride, that between the *Chesapeake* and HMS *Shannon.* Of the twenty-five known prints, only two were published in the United States and the others in England. The *Shannon*'s commander was knighted, pieces of plate were presented, and he was made the English hero of the war. The American commander, James Lawrence, came up with the famous phrase as he died, "Don't give up the ship," which has been used on numerous subsequent occasions.

Since the War of 1812 and up until the Civil War, there was very little call for prints. The action between the *Monitor* and the *Merrimac* renewed the national demand for naval scenes, but in the interval American taste declined the aquatints and the other forms of engravings and settled for lithographs and chromo-lithographs. The day of the top-grade printmakers was done.

M. V. Brewington
Kendall Whaling Museum
Sharon, Massachusetts

PREFACE

Several years ago, at the suggestion of a few friends and fellow print collectors, I began to compile information on American naval prints I had started to collect in the early 1950's. By so doing I found that I was giving myself a course in naval history, and not a very cheap one at that. Subsequently it occurred to me that there were very few sources of information on naval prints and perhaps no catalogues that offered the reader a chronological narrative tying in with the events depicted. Early in my collecting career I had decided to concentrate only on the American Navy under sail. This was basically an economic decision, but it also helped me avoid becoming a "jack of all trades, master of none." What evolved is a catalogue organized as an informal naval history.

In a collector's catalogue perhaps a touch of avarice is admissible. Thus, where noteworthy, mention will be made of degree of rarity, but price will be avoided, because of the imprecise nature of the market. Naval prints do not enjoy the wide popularity of antique furniture, silver, and porcelain. A really fine Philadelphia Queen Anne armchair, of which perhaps there are fifty or sixty extant, may fetch $25,000 or more, while one *Constellation* aquatint by Savage, of which there are only four known sets, may bring a third of that price.

"Excessive rarity," that trite expression, may mean just that. Alec Vietor, curator of prints at Yale, postulated a theory that rarity can reach the point of diminishing return. A paucity of supply might cause a paucity of demand, especially in an imperfect market such as exists for prints. On the other hand, there have been collectors of unusual influence, such as Presidents Franklin D. Roosevelt and John F. Kennedy, both of whom were ardent devotees of naval prints. Their influence tended to spur demand

In the case of important prints, the writer will attempt to trace their provenance in terms of previous ownership. Mention is made of those prints which came from the Francis Garvan collection, the Henry Graves collection, and the Havemeyer sale. Also noted are print numbers from the Olds catalogue and Grolier and Stauffer catalogues, if available.

The foremost collection of this sort was amassed by Irving Olds. His was the indirect inspiration for mine, although I had barely a speaking acquaintance with Mr. Olds before he died. His collection hung in the U. S. Steel Building in downtown Manhattan until his death, when it was transferred to the New-York Historical Society.

The original instigator of both Mr. Olds and, a generation later, myself, was Harry Shaw Newman of the Old Print Shop in New York. He had no peer in this field, although Rudolf G. Wunderlich of the Kennedy Galleries would have to be rated among the top today. Both of these gentlemen have impoverished me in the past. Occasionally I have found good things at Parker's Gallery in Albemarle Street in London, in the old days at Sessler's in Philadelphia, at Goodspeed's and Childs' in Boston, and of course at the periodic auctions that occur.

I am indebted to my wife, Peggy, who gradually yielded wall space and permitted me to pretend I was in her league in collecting Americana, furniture being her field of interest. Also, her father, the late Henry Belin du Pont, gave me encouragement to pursue this period of naval engravings which did not overlap his own fine collection of a later period, mostly centered around his wife's ancestor, Admiral S. F. du Pont, USN.

In addition to the historical aspects of a print collection, there is the matter of its various art forms: woodcut, mezzotint, stipple engraving, line engraving, aquatint, lithograph, and etching. This is not, however, the special expertise of the writer. A real connoisseur, like Lessing Rosenwald, could look at a print and tell whether the engraver's burin was dull when the lines were cut in his plates. Therefore, technical evaluation of this sort will be kept to a minimum. Emphasis will be rather on the events, together with a description of the collection, albeit a modest one at that. Others, far better qualified, have written on the subject of the art of engraving and have codified the engravers.

It should be noted that in this particular form of Americana, collectors include the work of foreign artists and engravers, as long as the subject matter is at least partly American. That is the criterion, whereas in American furniture the cabinet maker must be American and the object has to be made in America.

As might be expected, the product of the American engraver was not always as sophisticated as that of the English, particularly in hand-colored aquatints, where artisans such as R. and D. Havell, Robert Dodd, Joseph Jeakes, and Joseph Cartwright did such splendid work in Britain. On the other hand, Edward Savage in Philadelphia pioneered aquatints in America of nearly comparable quality to those of London.

In the field of line engraving, less sophisticated than aquatint, names such as William Birch, Samuel Seymour, Benjamin Tanner, and Cornelius

Tiebout in Philadelphia, Paul Revere and Abel Bowen in Boston, and Amos Doolittle in Connecticut were prominent.

Also in line engraving, Italy is represented by John B. Guerrazzi, who contributed handsomely to the portrayal of the Tripolitan War, which was of some importance to the Italian States.

The French, who were prominent in many forms of art, surprisingly did not contribute materially to early naval prints, with a few exceptions. However, with the advent of lithography they came to the fore: Perrot, Betremieux, and Debucourt—all rendering excellent work.

Lithography as an art form emerged after copper and steel engravings had their day. In this medium, Louis Haghe in London and Nathaniel Currier in the States were superior. In terms of sheer output, Nathaniel Currier and the successor firm of Currier and Ives were by far the most prolific. Since lithography was a later medium it is unlikely that any of the lithographs in this collection could have been produced contemporaneously with the events portrayed.

Authoritative books on these various media include Stauffer's *American Engravers upon Copper and Steel* and Mantle Fielding's *American Engravers upon Copper and Steel.* By far the best guide to the collector of naval prints is Irving S. Olds' *Bits and Pieces of American History,* published in 1952. Also useful is the Grolier Club catalogue of 1942 and the catalogues of sales which the Kennedy Galleries have published, most notably the one of the Graves collection. The recently published catalogue of J. William Middendorf II depicts prints of great significance and has excellent documentation.

As to artistic merits of individual prints, I will avoid comment for the most part, except as may have been made by Mr. Olds or by Harry Shaw Newman, for the simple reason that their opinions are more likely to be accurate. It takes no genius to note the condition, margins, or repairs of a print. On the other hand, to know the state, first or second strike, etc., requires more expertise. In most cases, where such information is stated, the writer will have relied on others. There are two sets of numbers to be found in the text, one referring to the plates in this book and the other referring to the prints themselves.

It should be noted that this is not intended as a textbook but rather as a collector's catalogue, together with appropriate historical commentary. At times I inject my own opinions; and the reader is thus forewarned.

* * *

Subsequent to the preparation of this text but too late for inclusion, I acquired four rare prints that have some naval connotation. Two are scenes of the Battle of Bunker Hill from the water, showing the British ships firing broadsides. One is by Bernard Romans and was published in Philadelphia in 1775. The other, also published in Philadelphia, is by Robert Aitken for the *Pennsylvania Magazine,* September 1775. The third print was engraved by John Bower in 1815 and depicts the bombardment of Fort McHenry in Baltimore. The fourth is a 1767 view of part of the city of Philadelphia, centered around the Pennsylvania Hospital. It was engraved by J. Hulett after a sketch by Nicholas Garrison, son of a sea captain and a resident of Philadelphia. To call this a naval print requires some stretch of the imagination. Many old sailors, however, ended their days at the nation's oldest hospital.

E. Newbold Smith

ACKNOWLEDGMENTS

During the course of this project, I was given assistance by certain people whom I wish to thank. Most importantly, I should express my appreciation to Bruce Inverarity, director of the Philadelphia Maritime Museum. He took an active interest in the preparation of my manuscript and guided it all the way through to the printing. He labored many hours over my raw material. He was also responsible for the choice of photographer, Bernard Aronson, whose transparencies were excellent.

I also wish to thank Edwin Wolf II, of the Library Company of Philadelphia, for his assistance; Jon Beckmann, Gail Stewart for her meticulous final editing; and Walter Tower of the Nimrod Press.

E. Newbold Smith

Chapter I

HISTORICAL PERSPECTIVE

Like other sciences, naval warfare advanced at a snail's pace for 2,000 years. Then with the advent of steel and steam it accelerated to the point where surface warfare became a thing of the past. But looking back over the skein of history, one is not hard put to select the really great sea episodes, which will be mentioned here for the purpose of putting the American experience in perspective. We must not, for example, put John Paul Jones above Lord Nelson or the USS *Bon Homme Richard* in a class with HMS *Victory*.

Initially, consider the Punic Wars (264-241 B.C.) between Rome and Carthage, won finally by Rome. These were military battles on the water, where the idea was to row one's galley alongside that of the enemy and board him with one's troops. The Battle of Actium, Octavius and Antony (31 B.C.), was fought largely with the same tactics, and again it was Rome over the Africans, in this case Cleopatra's Egyptians. Eighteen hundred years later Paul Jones employed precisely the same tactics to obtain victory over the *Serapis*.

In 1571, perhaps the most important naval battle of all time was fought to a deadly conclusion. This was the Battle of Lepanto, in the Adriatic, where the Allied Christian Fleet under Don Juan and Andrea Doria finally turned back the Ottoman Empire represented by the fleet of Ali Pasha. It was Christian versus Infidel, with many of the former rowing as slaves for the latter. No less than 150,000 men were locked in this titanic struggle to save the Western World for Christianity. The Pope himself had furnished a major part of the Allied Fleet. Tactics and equipment at Lepanto differed from that of the actions 1,600 years later only to a minor degree. The idea was to get alongside and board.

In 1588 there was the Spanish Armada and then in the late 1600's the Anglo-Dutch Wars, which were fought over the control of commerce. Then there was a series of wars between Britain and France which were classic examples of the struggle for seapower. The Battle of Saints Passage, fought in the West Indies in 1782 between Admiral de Grasse and Admiral Rodney, was of special significance. This culminated in the British takeover of the West Indies, but—much more important from a student's point of view—this battle was where the time-honored fighting instructions of the Duke of York were violated. Instead of arraying his squadron in line of procession and engaging the enemy in the so-called line of battle tactic, Rodney, perhaps inadvertently, isolated part of his French adversary, broke through his line, and "crossed his T," or, in military parlance, enfiladed him. Had Admiral Rodney not won such a tremendous victory, then surely he would have been court-martialed for adopting this new tactic, which by its very success became forever afterwards the midshipman's dream. Horatio Nelson, under Sir John Jervis, did the same at Cape St. Vincent; the Japanese did it at Tsushima, when they decimated the Russian fleet; and finally in the greatest naval battle in the history of the world, Leyte Gulf, the United States Seventh Fleet under Admiral Kincaid, part of Admiral Halsey's enormous armada, crossed the T of the Japanese in Surigao Strait. They did it with obsolete battleships that ran out of ammunition.

Other notable engagements include the Glorious First of June, Lord Howe over the French in 1794; the Battle of the Nile, where Nelson thwarted Napoleon's Mediterranean aspirations; Trafalgar, which sealed Napoleon to an inevitable land defeat; and of course the Battle of Jutland in World War I.

In all of these great events and many others, the significance was nearly always in their strategic result rather than the sinking of so many tons. While Nelson's men were doing "their duty for England" off Cadiz, the real beneficiary was Tommy Atkins in Wellington's infantry.

Naval actions from the American Revolution through the War of 1812 constitute a series of extraordinary adventures and individual heroics that have hardly been equalled and probably never will be in the future. With the advent of steam, the glorious age of the sailing warship gradually went down over the western horizon.

The main arena of warfare in America's early years was on land, but exploits on the sea were no less celebrated. There was a quality of chivalry about naval warfare which, together with America's success at it, gave the embryonic nation a sense of pride it so needed. It was the spirit of these battles that enchants: bloody yet genteel. On one occasion rival American and British commanders were even buried side by side on the coast of Maine. Along the English coast, some of the American captains were greatly admired for their bravery and their humane treatment of prisoners. One such captain had officers of the Royal Navy as his pallbearers.

Public interest in these naval exploits was especially strong along the Eastern seaboard, where foreign trade was an important element of commerce. Boston was a center of maritime activity, but, surprisingly, so were Philadelphia and Baltimore, especially the former, where Joshua Humphreys turned out frigates such as the *United States* and *Philadelphia.* Famous officers like John Barry, Gustavus Conyngham, Nicholas Biddle, Stephen Decatur, Charles Stewart, Richard Somers, James Biddle, Richard Dale, and William Bainbridge all made their homes in the Quaker City at one time or another.

Until 1800, Philadelphia was the nation's capital. When Thomas Jefferson was elected president in 1800, the attitude toward France took a sharp turn for the better and French style became fashionable in the American capital. The country swung away from the Washington-Adams Federalists, and for several years after the brief Quasi-War, French and American policies beat to the same metronome. This tended to reorient America's naval effort. As in the earlier Revolutionary period, the new nation was successful, in part at least because of the preoccupation of John Bull with France in both Europe and the West Indies.

In 1798, while the Federalists were still in power, Navy Secretary Benjamin Stoddert called for twelve ships of seventy-four guns and twelve frigates. The anti-Federalist faction, headed by Representative Albert Gallatin of Pennsylvania, aided by the demise of the French Directory in 1799, managed to dissuade Congress, and only a part of the ship request was actually authorized. As was often the case in those days, the government authorized construction for one war only to have delivery for another. Thus the scanty preparations before the turn of the century did provide some ships for the Tripolitan War and the War of 1812.

As to manpower for the Navy, the young country was richly endowed. American naval customs and traditions derived from the Royal Navy, but her personnel, mostly from the New England and Middle Atlantic states, had the added incentive of defense of the homeland, sustained as it were by the fresh air of freedom. The latter apparently was worth an entire deck of 32's.

Historians sometimes tend to ignore the part played by the Navy in America's victories over Britain, both in the Revolution and in the War of 1812. In both cases France's part was crucial; in the first instance directly, in the second indirectly. Naval forces played a major role in these struggles for permanent independence from Britain. The officers, seamen, and marines of those early days were thus a vital part of the American heritage.

The subject here is American naval history, but often the controlling factors were national policies and events on another continent and in other waters. Britain was the principal adversary, but she was involved in a worldwide struggle with France, Holland, and Spain in colonization and commerce. Whitehall's indifference toward her "bloody colonials" may be understandable in the light of the activities of her natural enemies. Her overestimate of the value of the West Indies, however, was a serious error exceeded only by the underestimate of her own American colonies.

Chapter II

COLONIAL PERIOD

The early settlers were more concerned about the danger on land—the Indians—than any threats from the sea. However, early records show the typical struggle over fishing rights, over which English and French colonists fought for years. The French, by reason of their early voyages of discovery and later success in the fisheries, concentrated their colonization in the North, starting soon after 1600. The English, who founded Virginia and Massachusetts shortly after 1600, gradually consolidated their territories from New England to the Carolinas and Georgia. In the Delaware Valley, the Swedes gave in and in 1644, the Dutch at New Amsterdam capitulated, as part of the Second Anglo-Dutch War. The mainland at that point was a three-tiered affair—the French in the North, the English in the middle, and the Spanish in the South. The Caribbean Islands were still to be contested.

Piracy was a flourishing occupation but the distinction between pirate and privateer was a fine one. In fact, pirate and national hero were at times indistinguishable. Toward the latter 1600's the famous Captain Kidd made numerous appearances on the coast of North America allegedly burying treasure at various locations.

The slave trade, surprisingly, dates back to 1620, when the first blacks were landed at Jamestown in British ships. Later, New England merchants engaged profitably in this trade, delivering their cargo to the Carolinas and Virginia. Perhaps most notorious as promoters of the slave trade were the Rhode Island merchants. Between 1698 and 1708, 103 vessels were built in Rhode Island and traded between New England, Africa, the West Indies, and the Southern colonies. They would export lumber and fish and return with molasses and slaves. By 1756, there were 4,489 slaves in Boston, to say nothing of the South. Curiously, not all slaves were black. In 1652, 275 Scotsmen, captured by the English in battle, were delivered and sold in Boston! Slavery was obviously more prevalent in the South because of climate and the need for agricultural labor. Ironically, a good case can be made that New England merchants were more responsible for this unsavory trade than the Southerners for whose plantations they were delivered.

During this colonial period, Britain derived major benefits from her American colonies, not the least of which were skilled seamen. American tar and timber, especially the live oak, were important raw materials upon which the Royal Navy depended. Britain's strategy to secure for herself a large part of North America was well-founded and certainly in her self-interest. As a means to this end, there occurred in this period one significant engagement—the attack of 1745 on Fort Louisbourg on the outer coast of Cape Breton Island, Nova Scotia. Here the French had erected fortifications costing six million dollars and twenty-five years of development. This fortress commanded the entrance through Cabot Strait to the Gulf of St. Lawrence, and thus had great strategic significance to the French colonizers of North America.

England had declared war on France in 1744, and by April, 1745, an expedition was formed to attack Fort Louisbourg. This force consisted of New England soldiers under Colonel Pepperell and a naval task force under Captain Tyng of the Massachusetts colonial marine. This force was joined by a squadron of the Royal Navy under Commodore Warren. After a siege of forty-seven days, Fort Louisbourg surrendered. This action was part of King George's War, and in the settlement—the Peace of Aix-la-Chapelle—in 1748, Fort Louisbourg was returned to the French. However, the loss of this great fortress and all of Acadia was only delayed for another decade, when in 1758, during the French and Indian War, another naval and military combination under Admiral Boscawen and Generals Amherst and Wolfe finally delivered the coup de grace. This last battle ended the French threat from the North until the colonies themselves seceded in 1776.

Plate 1

No. 1

A View of the Landing of the New England Forces in ye Expedition against Cape Breton, 1745.

When after a Siege of 40 days the Town and Fortress of Louisbourg and the important Territories thereto belonging were recover'd to the British Empire. The brave & Active Commodore Warren, since made Knight of the Bath & Vice Admiral of ye White commanded the British Squadron in this glorious Expedition. The Hon. Willm. Pepperell Esqr. (since Knighted) went a Voluntier & Commanded the New England Men who bravely offer'd their service and went as private Soldiers, in this hazardous but very glorious Enterprize.

Printed for John Bowles at the Black Horse in Cornhil, & Carrington Bowles next the Chapter House in St. Pauls Church Yard, London.

I. Stevens Pinxit. Brooks Sculp.

Plate 1 *Attack on Fort Louisbourg*

Line engraving. 19¼″ by 12¾″. Colored by hand.

State II. Very rare. Other imps.: Brown University (state I), Colonial Williamsburg (state I), John Carter Brown Library (state II), Yale University (state II), New-York Historical Society (state III), Girard Trust Bank (state III), U.S. Naval Academy—Beverly R. Robinson Collection (state III).

The first state of this print was published in August, 1747, by John and Carrington Bowles. The third state was published by Robert Wilkenson, who took over Bowles' business, some time after 1779. Fort Louisbourg was recaptured the second time during the French and Indian War, or Seven Year War, as it was known abroad. There is an engraving of this second action in the Olds collection. However, technically it is not American, since it was strictly an engagement between British and French.

Chapter III

REVOLUTION

In the seventeenth and eighteenth centuries England made the monumental mistake of taking her North American colonies for granted. The Navigation Acts of the mid 1600's, which limited cargoes from the colonies to British bottoms, were abrasive to America. Then during the reign of the incompetent monarch George III, a succession of unpalatable acts were imposed on the colonies, including the Stamp Acts, the duty on tea, and many other petty encroachments.

The first overt act of resistance occurred in 1772 near Rhode Island when a small packet ship, the *Hannah,* led a British schooner, the *Gaspe,* onto a sand bar off Newport. That night townspeople from Providence went out, attacked, burned, and sacked the schooner, taking her crew ashore.

In 1773, the famous Boston Tea Party took place, and in 1775 there were the battles of Lexington and Concord, after which Washington was appointed commander-in-chief. In that same year, a noteworthy action took place off the New England coast in which a Marbleheader, Captain Mugford, with a small armed vessel, the *Franklin,* intercepted a British ammunition ship, the *Hope,* and captured her, together with 1,500 barrels of powder, tools, guns, and many other valuable stores.

Plate 2 No. 2

Captn. James Mugford of the Schr. Franklin Continental Cruiser 1776

One of the heroic men with Thomas Russell, 1st Lieut. and 19 Officers and men from Marblehead who captured the armed British Transport Ship Hope, Ladened with Powder, implements of War and Pioneer Tools, destined for and in sight of the British Admiralty Fleet then in Nantasket Roads Novr. 1775. The scarcity of Powder was severely felt by the Continental Congress the procuring of it attracted their particular and constant attention, every encouragement had been held by them to the inhabitants of the Country, to engage in the manufacture thereof, no opportunity was neglected in importing, or seizing it from the Enemy. March 1776 Genl. Washington entered Boston in triumph, the British evacuated and embarked, and lay in Nantasket Roads, waiting the arrival of their Powder Ship—The enterprising and heroic Mugford, with Officers and men captured said Ship and transfered her with Cargo to the United States Commissary Genl. and Quarter Master, by the Continental Agent, Col. Jonathan Glover. This was One of the most valuable prizes during the Revolution, the principal and interest to 1854, Amounts to 1,349,343 15/100 Dollars! this and similar events produced the general voice "We will be free." Congress deliberately

Plate 2 *Portrait of Captain James Mugford*

and solemnly decided to declare it to the world; and the Declaration of Independence was agreed to in Congress on the 4th of July 1776. Who can estimate the real value of that capture?

Entered, according to Act of Congress, in the year 1854 by GLOVER BROUGHTON in the Clerk Office of the District Court of Massachusetts.

Under the vignette of Mugford: "L. H. Bradford & Co.'s Lith."
Lithograph 18" by 13¼". Colored.
Not in Olds. Grolier 207.

In October, 1775, Continental Congress passed resolutions creating a Marine Committee for the purpose of fitting out ships to intercept certain British transports which were supplying Boston and British outposts in what is now Canada. In December, 1775, Congress authorized thirteen ships to be built and also appointed a commander-in-chief and several captains. Esek Hopkins of Rhode Island was the first commander-in-chief of the American Navy. Dudley Saltonstall was appointed captain of the *Alfred*, Abraham Whipple captain of the *Columbus*, Nicholas Biddle captain of the *Andrea Doria*, and John B. Hopkins captain of the *Cabot*. The first lieutenants included a man born in Scotland called John Paul Jones, who was assigned to the *Alfred*. The first flag to be hoisted on an American warship was hoisted on the *Alfred* in the Delaware River by her first lieutenant, John Paul Jones. It is thought that this flag was the one with the pine tree and the rattlesnake coiled at its roots with the motto: "Don't Tread on Me."

The first ship to embark on a cruise of war was the sloop *Lexington*, 14-guns, under John Barry, a Philadelphian born in Ireland. He cleared the Delaware Capes early in 1776, closely followed by a squadron under Commodore (or Admiral) Hopkins bound for Nassau. On arrival in the Bahamas, Hopkins sent in the Marines, who captured New Providence Island and significant quantities of guns and ammunition. On their return trip in April, Hopkins' squadron attacked a British man-of-war, the *Glasgow*, 20-guns, but the latter escaped after doing considerable damage to the American ships. Hopkins' lack of zeal and his apparent ineptness in the episode led to his censure by Congress later in the year, and he never again put to sea in the Navy. In early 1777, he was dismissed from the service.

At approximately the same time, spring of 1776, the *Lexington* under Captain John Barry acquitted herself quite differently. She captured the armed tender *Edward* in a very spirited encounter off the Virginia Capes.

The fact that these actions took place before the Declaration of Independence raises some interesting points. British forces had seized colonial ships on ordinary commercial voyages and had even sacked and burned the town of Falmouth, which is now Portland, Maine. So in November, 1775, Congress ordered the naval forces, such as they were, to interdict the supply of British garrisons on the American coast. This of course was war, declaration or no declaration.

Plate 3

No. 3

Hopkins Commandant en Chef la Flotte Américaine.

Dupin Sculp.

A Paris chez Esnauts et Rapilly, rue St Jacques à la Ville de Coutances A.P.D.R.

Half-length portrait with cocked hat on head. Beneath the portrait is a cannon, sword, and shield with flags draped on top. One flag says, "Don't tread upon me." The other flag says, "Liberty tree an appeal to God."

Line engraving. 6″ by 4¼″. Black and white. Undated.

Olds 453. Grolier 255.

No. 4

Commodore John Barry

Stuart pinx. Edwin sc.

Full bust portrait in uniform, without hat. Face toward right.

Stipple engraving. Oval 3⅞″ by 3¼″. Colored by hand. Undated.

Stauffer 711. Grolier 237. Olds 441.

Later during the affair with Algiers, John Barry was the first captain to be commissioned in the United States Navy. His commission, No. 1, was signed by Washington on 22 February, 1797, to take effect retroactively to 4 June, 1794. He had commanded the *Lexington* at the outbreak of the Revolution.

Plate 3 *Portrait of Commodore Hopkins*

Plate 4 *The Phoenix and the Rose*

Plate 4

No. 5

The Phoenix and the Rose Engaged by the Enemy's Fire Ships and Galleys on the 16 Augst. 1776.

Engrav'd from the Original Picture by D. Serres from a Sketch of Sir James Wallace's.

Publish'd according to Act of Parliament April 2, 1778 by J.F.W. Des Barres, Esqr.

Aquatint. 20″ by 11″. Colored by hand. First state, without palisades. The proof print had no lettering below the print. The second state has the palisades.

Very rare in any state. Other impressions: Harvard Club (state II); Augustus P. Loring (2 imps. state I, state II); Mariners Museum (state II); Carnegie Institute Museum (state II); National Maritime Museum, Greenwich, England (2 imps. state I, 2 imps. state II); New-York Historical Society (state I, state II); N.Y. Public Library (state II); Yale University (state II); U.S. Naval Academy, Beverly R. Robinson Collection (state II). Grolier 1(a). Olds 65 (state II).

This is an important print, not so much to the historian as to the collector. It is in perfect condition and to my knowledge no state of this has come on the market since this one was sold to J. William Middendorf II in the Graves Sale of 1959.

No. 6

The Phoenix and the Rose engaged by the Enemy's Fire Ships & Galleys on the 16th. Augt. 1776. Engraved from the Original Picture by D. Serres, from a sketch of Sir James Wallace's.

Lith. by G. Hayward, 171 Pearl St., N.Y., for D.T. Valentine's Manual, 1776.

This is a lithograph published in New York in 1864 for a city documentary. The publishing date on the plate is in error.

In July, 1776, HMS *Phoenix* and *Rose* anchored in the Hudson River off the palisades near the location of the present George Washington Bridge. On 16 August, 1776, a group of patriots, using fire ships, tried to destroy these enemy men-of-war but to no avail, except that they were able to force them to drop downstream. This was not a major action, but a print was published for use of the Royal Navy to illustrate and chronicle the event.

LANDING OF BRITISH ON LONG ISLAND
22 AUGUST, 1776

Plate 5

No. 7

Ontscheeping der Engelsche Troepen op Lang-Eiland Teegen de Americaanen, den 22 Augustus 1776.

B. Mourik excudit. In de Mercurius May 1777. Eerste Stuk, Pag. 156.

Line engraving on steel. 6⅜″ by 5⅛″. Black and white.

Most unusual. Ex F. S. Hicks collection. Not in Olds, Stauffer, Fielding or Grolier.

This engraving is interesting, as it shows that Hollanders conceived of New Amsterdam as tropical. Note the palm tree. Perhaps some early Dutch settlers complained about the hot summer? Also, in the upper part of the print in the background Boston is placed erroneously between New York and Philadelphia. Never has the writer seen this print elsewhere. It came from the collection of the late Hon. Frederick Hicks, U.S. Representative from 1st District of New York.

No. 8

Disembarkation of the Troops at Gravesend Bay under the Command of Sir George Collier, R.N. Baily Sculp.

London, Published 30 Novr. 1814, by Joyce Gold, at the Naval Chronicle Office, 103, Shoe Lane.

Stipple engraving. Vignette 9¼″ by 4¾″. Hand colored. One of a pair with *Sir George Collier's victory in Penobscot Bay.*
Olds 66.

In actuality the landing on Long Island was not an American naval proceeding. The troops were landed as part of General Howe's plan to capture New York from General Washington. Five days after the landing the Battle of Long Island was fought and lost by the Continentals, forcing Washington to abandon lower New York to the British.

Plate 5 *Landing of English Troops on Long Island*

Plate 6 *Arnold's Engagement on Lake Champlain*

ENGAGEMENT ON LAKE CHAMPLAIN
11-13 OCTOBER, 1776

Plate 6

No. 9

References. No. 1. Inflexible Ship. 2. Carleton Schooner. 3. Maria Schooner. 4. Congress Galley, run a Shore, with other Vessels a blowing up. 5. Washington Galley strikeing. 6. Gun Boat coming up.

London, Printed for Robt. Sayer & Jno. Bennett, No. 53, Fleet Street, as the Act directs, 22d. Decr. 1776.

Line engraving. 13¾″ by 9⅝″. Colored by hand. Artist and engraver unknown.
Grolier 2. Olds 67. Rare.

This battle between hastily erected vessels on Lake Champlain was unusual in that an army officer, General Benedict Arnold, commanded the American flotilla. Though it was a tactical victory for Britain, Arnold's fierce resistance delayed the intended invasion from Canada until the winter made it too late. One interesting note is that the officer commanding the vessel HMS *Carleton* was Lieutenant James Dacres. He distinguished himself in close combat in this action, and later, in the War of 1812, Dacres had command of HMS *Guerriere* in her famous battle with the USS *Constitution.*

General Benedict Arnold, in the writer's opinion a brilliant soldier who would have gone down in American military history second only to Washington had he not turned traitor, was the same officer who engineered the defeat of Burgoyne at Saratoga in October, 1777. That battle is generally regarded as the most significant of the entire war, as it thwarted the British attempt to cut off New England from the rest of the colonies. This great victory took place exactly one year after Arnold's lake engagement, sometimes known as the Battle of Valcour Island, and under identical strategic circumstances.

After General Arnold was wounded in the leg at Saratoga, Washington, thinking he needed some rest, put him in charge of the garrison at Philadelphia. Lord Howe had departed and the patriots took control of the city. At this point, two interesting things occurred. Lord North made overtures of peace, and the moderate Tories, of which there were many in Philadelphia, felt that the war should end and the colonies should reestablish ties to Britain. Philadelphia was the capital, and one can imagine the leaders of the city gossiping on the merits of this proposition versus an alliance with Roman Catholic France. Arnold, at thirty-five, always a favorite of the ladies, had lost his first wife and was courting twenty-year-old Peggy Shippen, the stunning daughter of a moderate Tory. On top of this influence, Arnold always had his difficulties with Congress, which he felt had never treated him well. Then, too, diplomacy was not one of his virtues. This was the general background but certainly not the justification for his fateful decision to go over to the British side. The story of his later clandestine moves while at West Point, involving the dashing Major John André as the enemy's courier, is one of history's favorite arcane events. During the British occupation André had also courted Peggy Shippen. When he was caught inside American lines and executed as a spy, he became instantly the English equivalent of Nathan Hale.

MUD FORT ACTION

After General Howe occupied Philadelphia in 1777, shipping in the Delaware was put into a state of disarray. In support of Howe, the British took steps to seize control of the entire river. They assembled a small fleet of light draught vessels, headed by HMS *Augusta,* 64-guns, and proceeded to lay siege to Fort Mifflin, situated on Mud Island below Philadelphia. In the course of this action, the Pennsylvania Navy under Commodore Hazelwood employed fire vessels against the enemy fleet, which included the *Augusta, Roebuck, Pearl, Isis, Liverpool,* and the sloop *Merlin.* Both the *Augusta* and *Merlin* caught fire and were abandoned and grounded on Hog Island. The British were repulsed in this battle, but eventually the fort fell.

The hulks of the two British vessels remained for years on the banks of Hog Island, which later belonged to Edgar Newbold Black, whose grandfather General John Black was a paymaster in Washington's army. Captain William Bispham Black, to whom, together with the writer's father, this work is dedicated, was a grandson of the Hog Island Black and the writer is his great grandson. Black's farmhouse had been hit by a cannon ball intended for the fort. Thus, in the Black family records the property was called Cannon Ball Farm.

Plate 7 No. 10

Drawn on the Spot & Engraved by Lieut. W. Elliott.

Representation of the Action off Mud Fort in the River Delaware the Enemys fleet consisting of Frigates, Fire ships, Galleys, &c. attacking His Majesty's Ships: Augusta, Roebuck Pearl, Liverpool and Merlin Sloop on the 22 of Octr. 1777 In which the Augusta took fire by Accident and the Merlin was burnt to prevent her falling into the hands of the Enemy.

London. Publish'd by W. Elliott 71 Park Street 17th. of Febr. 1787.

Aquatint. 20⅝" by 17¾". Black and white.

Of the greatest rarity, in fact unique. The most important print in the collection. The late I. N. Phelps Stokes records only three known impressions. One print was in his collection, which is now in the New York Public Library. One impression was in the Graves collection; however, it was purchased in 1959 by Mr. Olds after *Bits and Pieces* had already been published and is now in the New-York Historical Society print collection. The third, illustrated here, was acquired by the late Adolph Rosengarten of Philadelphia. The writer is indebted to his son, Adolph Rosengarten, Jr., for this one item which had eluded him for twenty-one years. The print is framed in oak from timber from the hulk of HMS *Augusta,* one of the two ships which were destroyed in the action. The engraving has been in this unique frame since sometime in the 1800's, as evidenced by the style of mat, according to Miss Mabel Zahn of Sessler's.

Close examination of the three known copies of this engraving discloses the following:

They were produced in London not Philadelphia, as Mr. I. N. Phelps Stokes asserted. They are all different, but the only difference between the Graves/Olds copy in the New-York Historical Society and the above copy is that the Graves copy is colored. The Graves copy has some tears but otherwise is in good condition. The above copy is pristine with full margins, very remarkable for a print of this age. The Stokes copy omits the word "Sloop" after Merlin and has an incorrect date—15th November 1777—for the action. The publication line of the Stokes copy in the New York Public Library is totally different, reading: "Published as the Act directs by W. Elliott in Park

Plate 7 *Action off the Mud Fort in the River Delaware*

Street 17th of Feby. 1787." Dimensions of each differ, but that is not unusual. The Graves copy is 20 ¾" by 17 ⅞", whereas the above is 21" by 17 ⅞".

A possible explanation for the extreme scarcity of this print is that the painter and engraver, William Elliott, was an officer of the Royal Navy. A lieutenant at the time of the action, he later became a captain, which indicates he made the Navy a permanent career. He died at Leeds, England, in 1792. Since he was a regular officer, it is improbable that he published commercially, but he may have produced a minimum number of engravings for friends.

Only one print in the entire collection (plate 34) can match the Mud Fort engraving for rarity, and none can match it for historical relevance both to the Revolution and to the writer's family and home.

WAR OFF THE ENEMY'S SHORES

In the fall of 1776, a 16-gun brig, the *Reprisal,* under the command of Captain Lambert Wickes, conveyed Dr. Benjamin Franklin to his post in France. During this cruise she captured two of the enemy's ships and, shortly after landing Franklin at Nantes, she captured two more. The American commissioners in France immediately saw the value of carrying the war to Britain's homeland by harassing her coasts, intercepting her commerce, and most important, if possible, cutting her supply lines to America. In the spring of 1777, Captain Lambert Wickes of the *Reprisal,* who had been joined by Captain Henry Johnston of the *Lexington,* managed two circuits of Ireland, creating great havoc and making several captures which were secretly disposed of in France, then officially neutral.

Having seen the success of such bold ventures, Congress authorized America's agents in France to purchase vessels to carry the war further along the British coasts. One such craft, the *Surprise,* was outfitted in France and put under the command of Captain Gustavus Conyngham, an Irish American of exceptional daring and skill.

After Conyngham had made several captures, he became something of a problem to his French hosts, who were not yet prepared for another war with Britain. At one point, the British, who regarded him as a rank pirate, sent two ships across the Channel to take Conyngham back for imprisonment. However, he escaped and secured another ship, the *Revenge.*

The cruise of the *Revenge* around the British coasts was amazingly successful, as she took prizes almost daily, sending them to France and Spain to be sold for foreign exchange to aid the young Republic. Conyngham's daring was such that on one occasion he disguised his identity and entered a British port for a complete refit and overhaul! Such feats forced insurance rates to unprecedented heights.

The total number of British merchant vessels sunk or captured by authorized cruisers and by privateers during 1777 was 467.

No. 11

*Een Engelsche Paket-boot door een Americaansche Kaaper genoomen, den 2 May A*o. *1777.*

H. Kobell inv. S. Fokke sc.

A. Fokke simonsz Excudit.

Line engraving. 3 15/16″ by 3″. Undated. Black and white.
Very rare. Not in Olds or Grolier.

This depicts the capture of the cross channel packet *Prince of Orange* on 3 May, 1777, not 2 May as print says, by the Continental luggar *Surprise* under Captain Gustavus Conyngham.

In 1778, John Paul Jones appeared in the same area with *Ranger,* 18-guns, and his exploits surpassed the feats of Conyngham. He ranged up and down the Irish Sea, off the coasts of Scotland and even landed, set fire to shipping, and captured forts. In one major action he captured HMS *Drake,* 20-guns, and took her as a prize to France.

The next year Jones attained a much better command, the *Bon Homme Richard.* With this vessel and several others commanded by French nationals under American auspices, he set sail for a cruise around the British Isles. After several encounters, all to his credit, he fell in with HMS *Serapis* and *Countess of Scarborough.*

The battle that ensued is famous in naval annals. The two ships, the *Bon Homme Richard,* 42-guns, and HMS *Serapis,* 50-guns, hammered away at close quarters, even locked together for 3 hours and 30 minutes. Finally the Americans, who controlled the decks by the superiority of their marines in the topmasts, by the lucky heave of a grenade that exploded on the gun deck of the *Serapis,* and the leadership of Captain Jones and his First Lieutenant Richard Dale, managed to force the gallant Captain Pearson to surrender. Casualties were exactly the same on both ships and, for a single action, enormous. Over a third of each ship's complement were killed or wounded.

Paul Jones' victory is made even more remarkable by the fact that the *Bon Homme Richard* was a converted merchantman, not very seaworthy, and the *Serapis* was a new 44-gun frigate. In addition, Jones' crew included about six different nationalities, and below decks she was loaded with prisoners. Lastly, Jones was deserted by his subordinate French captains, one of whom, Pierre Landais in the *Alliance,* actually fired several volleys into the *Bon Homme Richard.*

The exploits of John Paul Jones were so numerous and his achievements so great, it is no wonder that he is accorded the premier position among all the naval heroes of the United States. He was to the American Navy what Lord Nelson became to the Royal Navy: a legend in his own lifetime.

No. 12

Paul Jones American. Capitaine Commandant la Fregatte l'Alliance Celebre par son intrepidite dans les Combats.

Line engraving. Colored by hand. 7 15/16″ by 6 5/16″. Artist, engraver, and publisher unknown and undated.
Not in Olds or Grolier.

Irving S. Olds wrote an article in the magazine *Antiques* in December, 1959, about this print and its companion piece, which follows. He asserts that 1780 was the date of issuance.

Plate 8 No. 13

Augustatus Kuningam Fameux Marin Comodore au Service des Etats unis de l'Amerique et la terreur des Anglois.

Figure 65 at top.
Line engraving. Colored by hand. 10½″ by 6 15/16″. Companion to No. 12.
Very rare. Not in Olds or Grolier.

Plate 8 *Portrait of Gustavus Conyngham*

Plate 9 *Portrait of John Paul Jones*

Plate 9

No. 14

Iohann Paul Iones, Befehlshaber einer Schwadron in Diensten Der 13, Vereinigten Provinzen Von Nord-Amerika. 1779.

I E Haid Sculp.

Zu finden in Augsburg bey J. J. Haid u Sohn.

Mezzotint. 12¼″ by 9⅝″. Black and white. Undated. It is believed this was published in Augsburg in 1780. Engraved by Johann Elias Haid.
Olds 459. Grolier 265.

Plate 10

No. 15

The memorable Engagement of Captn. Pearson of the Serapis, with Paul Jones of the Bon Homme Richard & his squadron, Sep. 23. 1779. Combat mémorable donné le 22 7bre. 1779, entre le Capitaine Pearson commandant Le Serapis, et Paul Jones commandant Le Bon-Homme-Richard & Son Escadre.

To Sir Richard Pearson Knt. whose Bravery and Conduct saved the Baltic Fleet, under his Convoy tho' obliged to submit to a much superior force, This representation of that Action, Is with great Respect Inscribed, by his most obedient Servant, Richard Paton.

J. Boydell excudit 1781.

Richd Paton Pinxit. Lerpiniere & Fittler Sculpnt.

Published Decr. 12th. 1780, by John Boydell, Engraver in Cheapside, London.

The armament of the respective ships is spelled out in detail in English on the left and in French on the right.
Line engraving. Black and white. 23″ by 17⅜″.
Olds 74. Grolier 5.

Plate 11

No. 16

To the Merchants trading to Russia, this Print representing the gallant Defence of Captn. Pearson in his Majesty's Ship Serapis, and the Countess of Scarborough Arm'd Ship Captn. Piercy, against Paul Jones's Squadron, whereby a valuable Fleet from the Baltic were prevented from falling into the hands of the Enemy, is with the greatest respect Inscribed by their Humble Servant John Harris.

Plate 10 *Bon Homme Richard and Serapis*

Plate 11 *Serapis and Countess of Scarborough engaging Squadron of John Paul Jones*

Following is a description of the engagement:

This desperate Action was fought the 23 Sepr. 1779 off Scarborough, the Serapis for three hours sustaining a very unequal Fight, having the Bon Homme Richard fast locked alongside by the sheet Anchor hooking his Mizen Chains; at the same time the Alliance sailing round them pouring in her Broadsides raking her Fore & Aft without their being able to bring a Gun to bear upon her, more than half her people killed & wounded, & several times on Fire, was forced to submit. The Countess of Scarborough engaged the Pallas but having 7 Guns dismounted, her Sails and Rigging much wrecked she struck to a superior Force.

Robt. Dodd, Pinxit. J. Peltro, Fecit.

London Publish'd 1 Decr. 1781, by John Harris, Sweetings Alley Cornhill.

On each side of the description of the battle is a notation of the armament of the ships, the English force on the left, the American on the right.

Line engraving. 17⅜″ by 12″. Colored by hand.

Olds 76. Grolier 6.

As might be expected, the wording of this English engraving puts Captain Pearson in a rather better light than American texts would have us believe. It doesn't mention the fact that the *Alliance* raked the *Bon Homme Richard* as well as the *Serapis.* It also put the casualties higher than they were. However, it does play up the tactical fact that Pearson's fight did save the merchantmen from capture. Captain Pearson was a very brave officer and was held in esteem in the Royal Navy. Captain Landais of the *Alliance* was later dismissed from the service. He was spared the firing squad only by the question of his sanity.

Plate 12 No. 17

Combat Mémorable donné le 22 7bre. 1779, entre le Capitaine Pearson commandant le Sérapis, et Paul Jones commandant le Bon-Homme-Richard et son Escadre.

After this inscription is a statement in French of the armament, crew, and casualties on each ship, then a general description of the engagement.

A Paris chez Mondhare et Jean rue St. Jean de Beauvais, No. 4.

Artist and engraver not stated. It is believed that this is after Richard Paton's painting, with the view reversed. The date of the engagement in this print is inaccurate.

Line engraving. 19¼″ by 12⅜″. Colored by hand. Undated.

Grolier No. 9. Similar to Olds 76 with different publisher.

Plate 12 *Memorable Combat between Serapis and Bon Homme Richard*

Plate 13 *Paul Jones' Attack*

The Francis Garvan collection had this print in black and white. According to the Grolier catalogue the Garvan impression was an earlier state than the Olds. The above print is the same as the Garvan copy except colored. The coloring appears original and the condition of the print is mint. It came from the collection of the late Henry Havemeyer.

Plate 13 No. 18

Paul Jones. Attaque une flotte Anglaise commandée par Pearson, revenant de la Baltique en 1793.

Dessiné et Lith. par Ferd. Perrot.

Lith. Rigo fs. et Cie. r Richer, 7.

Paris, Chez Victor Delarue et Cie. E 75 Place du Louvre, 10.

Lithograph. 16 5/16″ by 11¼″. Undated. Colored by hand.

This print actually is Grolier 11A; Henry Havemeyer lent it to the Grolier Club in November 1942. The date of the engagement in this print is also inaccurate, it having occurred on 23 September, 1779.

Plate 14 No. 19

Combat engagé entre deux vaisseaux Anglais et deux Frégates des Etats-Unis d'Amérique.

Dessiné et lith. par Ferd Perrot.

Paris. publié par Vor. Delarue & Cie. Place du Louvre, 10

Imprimé par Lemercier, à Paris.

Victor Delarue's water mark is imprinted above the publisher's line.

Lithograph. 17″ by 11¼″. Colored by hand. Undated.

This is one of a group of Ferdinand Perrot lithographs of the action between Paul Jones' squadron and that of Sir Richard Pearson. This one is similar to Olds 83, but not quite the same in the lettering. In fact the publishers are different.

Plate 15 No. 20

Combat Naval

Ferdd. Perrot.

Lithograph. 16¾″ by 11⅝″. Colored by hand. Not dated and not otherwise lettered, except "No. 30" at the top.

Plate 14 *Engagement between Two English Vessels and Two American Frigates*

Plate 15 *Naval Combat*

Not in Olds or Grolier. This came from the collection of Henry Havemeyer and represents action between *Bon Homme Richard* and *Serapis*.

Plate 16

No. 21

Épisode de la Guerre de L'Indépendance

Dessiné et Lith. par Ferd. Perrot.

Lith. Coulon, r. richer, 7.

Paris. chez Victor Delarue, Editeur, Place du Louvre, 10.

Lithograph. 16¾″ by 11⅜″. Colored by hand. Undated.
Olds 86. This is Grolier 210, lent by the late Henry Havemeyer.

This is a most interesting view of the *Bon Homme Richard-Serapis* engagement, for in the foreground are two life boats swarming with men struggling, one boat against the other. It is known that at the battle's end certain prisoners on board the *Richard* stole a ship's boat off the *Serapis* and made for shore. This may account for the artist's featuring of the action in the small boats.

No. 22

John Paul Jones, Commodore au Service des Etats-Unis de l'Amérique, tel qu'il était dans le combat du 23 7bre. 1779 contre le Co͞modore Pearson, son Vaisseau le bon ho͞me Richard montait 40 canons. Le Vaisseau Anglais Le Serapis 44, avait encore l'avantag du calibre, et la legèrté. Le Co͞modore P. Jones, par sa maneuvre engagea le Beaupré de l'e͞nemi, et s'empara du Serapis en le combattant bord à bord pandant 2 heures 3/4. l'Action dura 3 heures et 1/4. Le bon homme Richard coula le lendemain.

Dessiné par C:J:Notté Gravé par Carl Guttenberg.

à Paris chez Guttenberg rue St. Hyacinthe la 2me. porte par la place St. Michel.

Line engraving. 10⅞″ by 9¼″. Black and white. Undated.
Olds 462. Grolier 264.

Plate 17

No. 23

Paul Jones shooting a Sailor who had attempted to strike his Colours in an Engagement.

From the Original Picture by John Collet, in the possession of Carrington Bowles.

Printed for & Sold by Carrington Bowles, at his Map & Print Warehouse, No. 69 in St. Paul's Church Yard, London.

Published as the act directs, 2d. Decr. 1779.

Mezzotint. 12⅞″ by 9 15/16″. Black and white. The number 411 is printed in lower left corner.

Olds 366, Grolier 269, except not colored.

Plate 18

No. 24

Capt. Paul Jones shooting a Sailor who had attempted to strike his Colours in an Engagement.

London, Printed for R. Sayer & J. Bennett, Map & Printsellers, No. 53, Fleet Street, as the Act directs, 1st. Jany. 1780.

Mezzotint. 12⅞″ by 9⅞″. Colored by hand. Artist and engraver unnamed. Olds 367. Grolier 268.

Since Jones was such a terror to the English nation, no effort was spared to characterize him as a rogue. There is no known evidence that such an incident took place.

Plate 19

No. 25

Naval Heroes of the United States. No. 3. Bon Homme Richard and Serapis.

Oval portraits of John Paul Jones, Alexander Murray, Richard Dale, Nicholas Biddle, John Barry and Edward Preble around view in center of the engagement between the *Bon Homme Richard* and the *Serapis.*

Lith & Pub. by N. Currier, 2 Spruce St. N.Y.

Entered according to Act of Congress in the year 1846 by N. Currier, in the Clerk's office of the District Court of the Southern District of N.Y.

Lithograph. 12¾″ by 9⅜″. Colored by hand. "No. 3" in lower right corner. Grolier 12. H. T. Peters' Currier & Ives 1938. Olds 491.

No. 26

Destruction of the Randolph Frigate.

Artist, engraver and publisher unnamed.

Line engraving. 4¼″ by 2⅝″. Black and white. Undated.

Plate 16 *Episode of the War of Independence*

Plate 17 *Paul Jones Shooting a Sailor*

This is believed to have been an illustration from an unidentified history of North America, published in London, 1789. The Continental frigate *Randolph,* 32-guns, was commanded by Nicholas Biddle, who had made several successful cruises, especially out of Charleston. She was overwhelmed by the 64-gun ship-of-the-line *Yarmouth,* under Captain Nicholas Vincent, R.N., on 7 March, 1778, about 180 miles east of Barbados in the West Indies. Biddle, aged twenty-seven, went down with his ship. Two years earlier, Captain Biddle had command of the *Andrew Doria,* one of the ships in Commodore Esek Hopkins' squadron, which was the first fleet to go to sea for the United States. They started from the foot of Walnut Street, Philadelphia, in January, 1776, but were detained by ice off Reedy Island in the Delaware and finally cleared the Delaware Capes in February. *Andrew Doria* was in Hopkins' squadron in the attack on New Providence Island, Bahamas. Paul Jones was first lieutenant on the flagship *Alfred,* as previously mentioned.

No. 27

Sir George Collier's victory in Penobscot Bay 1779.

Baily Sculp. Published Novr. 1, 1814, by Joyce Gold, Naval Chronicle Office, 103, Shoe Lane, London.

Aquatint. Oval 9¼″ by 5″. Hand colored. Illustration from Vol. XXXII of *The Naval Chronicle,* published in London, 1814.
Olds 73. Grolier 4.

From an American point of view, the best that can be said of this episode is that it was botched. It seems that when General Gage left Boston, the State of Massachusetts decided it was time to recapture control of Penobscot Bay, then part of the State. The British had a base at Castine. Instead of coordinating efforts with federal authorities, for some reason the State decided to attack Castine with its own militia and a hastily assembled naval force. Captain Saltonstall was put in charge of the naval vessels and a group of privateers. Secrecy was not one of their virtues, and soon after the task force arrived at Castine, Sir George Collier appeared in HMS *Rainbow,* 64-guns, with four other vessels. The American expedition was quickly scattered and the whole affair ended in the chase and destruction of the State's forces.

Plate 18 *Capt. Paul Jones Shooting a Sailor*

Plate 19 *Naval Heroes of the United States*

No. 28

Alliance and Atalanta

Woodcut. 5¾" by 3½". Colored by hand. Undated. Artist and engraver unstated.

On 31 March, 1781, Captain Barry, having made an Atlantic passage to France, carrying important personnel, cleared L'Orient in the company of a French letter of marque, the *Marquis de la Fayette.* After three days out they captured two privateers, but after that the *Alliance* proceeded alone. On 28 May two brigs bore down on her as the wind was going flat. The smaller vessels had the advantage in light air and poured broadside after broadside into the *Alliance* while she had no steerageway.

Barry was wounded and carried below. Just as things looked hopeless the wind piped up and the *Alliance* sprang to the attack. In short order she managed to overcome her smaller adversaries, one of which was the 16-gun brig *Atalanta.* The *Alliance* made port safely, but her prize was recaptured on her way to Boston.

DELAWARE BAY

In 1782, the merchants of Philadelphia were becoming exasperated with the activities in the lower part of the Delaware River and Bay, where enemy cruisers preyed on American shipping. To rectify this, the Commonwealth of Pennsylvania undertook the forming of a squadron to purge the river of such a nuisance.

A small ship, the *Hyder Ally*, was purchased and Lieutenant Joshua Barney of the Navy was procured as her captain. She was a shoal draught merchantman, ideal for the Delaware. She was pierced for 16 six-pounders and a crew of 110 men were put aboard. Her first duty was to escort a convoy down the Delaware. On arrival off Cape May the convoy anchored to await a wind shift. At that point two ships and a brig rounded the Cape and came in to attack.

By the combination of shoal waters, which grounded one of the enemy, and superior maneuvering, Barney managed to capture the enemy force and thus protect his convoy. His victory against HMS *General Monk,* 20 nine-pounders, was clearly one of the feats of the war. Surely, local knowledge must have been available to the Americans, for Delaware Bay is frightful to navigate, with its shoals and currents, even with modern aids to navigation.

Congress, for some reason, never gave Barney recognition, and later in 1795 when the senior naval list was published he was placed under Silas Talbot. Talbot was an army officer who served a term in Congress, and Barney resigned rather than serve as junior to him. Such were the jealousies.

No. 29

Commodore Barney

Wood, Pinx^t. *Childs & Gimber, Sc^t.*

Stipple engraving. Oval vignette 5″ by 4″.
Stauffer 340. Olds 234.

No. 30

Hole in the Wall—Island of Abaco

Wells Sculp.

Published 30 June, 1803 by J. Gold, 103 Shoe Lane.

Aquatint. Vignette. 8 3/16″ by 4¾″. Black and white.
An illustration from *The Naval Chronicle,* London, January-June 1803, Volume IX. This shows a British revenue cutter searching a suspected American smuggler off the Island of Abaco in the Bahamas.

There were many other naval actions and combination military-naval campaigns which, if this were purely a history text, might be included. However, the collection is lacking in certain items; probably no collection is ever complete. Furthermore, it might be noted that not one single engraving of the Revolutionary War's naval events was done in America. A few engravers were active in the colonies, such as Revere, Aitkin, Doolittle, Romans, and Burgis. However, their subjects were rarely of a nautical nature.

Another factor that limited the actions of the period was the French Alliance of 1779, which changed the character of the war and put more American reliance on the French Navy. This invited the Royal Navy to the American shore in even greater force and brought a gradual diminution in American naval efforts and indeed in warfare on the sea. After the Battle of Saratoga in late 1777, the war scene on the American continent gradually shifted to the South, where operations were characterized more by the movement of armies.

Still, as in the later campaigns of Napoleon, control of the sea was crucial. In October, 1781, at Yorktown, the sea belonged to Admiral deGrasse. On the very day that Cornwallis surrendered, Sir Henry Clinton set sail from New York with twenty-five ships-of-the-line, ten frigates, and 7,000 troops. In five days he was at the mouth of the Chesapeake, but that was five days too late for history.

Chapter IV

FEDERAL PERIOD AND QUASI-WAR

After peace was signed in 1783, through the Articles of Confederation, and well into Washington's term as president, the young nation concerned itself with domestic affairs, Indian matters, taxes, and nearly everything except a navy.

As early as 1785, four years before the Union, Algerian corsairs attacked and captured American merchantmen, putting the seamen in irons. A maritime country without a navy was ideal prey for the Dey of Algiers. In 1792, Washington appointed John Paul Jones, who was restively unoccupied in Paris, as special agent or consul to negotiate with Algiers. Unfortunately, the great officer was dead before his commission to that post arrived.

The depredations of these pirates continued, indeed well out into the Atlantic Ocean. By 1794, Congress finally authorized the building of a navy, over the objections, incidentally, of the then liberal party, the Republicans (now the Democrats). The Federalists, or conservative party in power, favored the establishment of a navy, which was natural in that most maritime states were Federalist. One Republican representative, Albert Gallatin of Pennsylvania, was the bête noir to naval legislation, resisting it relentlessly. Henry Knox, Washington's former general and then secretary of war, together with Representative William L. Smith of Charleston and the New England contingent, were the navy's protagonists, but the most effective support came in the form of further pirate outrages. This strengthened the Federalists' argument, whereas recurring peace overtures reinforced Republican views.

This legislative dispute was basically between isolationists and internationalists, the former faction being dominated by the liberal side, an interesting contrast to similar disputes prior to American entry in World War II. If there is any lesson to this lack of political consistency it would be, simply: self-interest, not philosophy, is what usually dictates. States concerned with development of the West or agriculture of the South could not care much about a handful of seamen in North African dungeons and probably even less about the shipowners of Boston and Salem.

In any case, the provocations were such that a construction programme was authorized. Initially, six frigates were to be built at the following locations:

United States	44 guns	Philadelphia
President	44 guns	New York

Constitution	44 guns	Boston
Constellation	38 guns	Baltimore
Chesapeake	38 guns	Portsmouth, Va.
Congress	38 guns	Portsmouth, N.H.

All of these ships were eventually built, but in the meantime a treaty was signed with the Dey of Algiers at the end of 1795. Since Congress had no surplus of funds, the programme was immediately slashed in half. Surviving were the *United States, Constitution,* and *Constellation.*

The construction programme was to be carried out under the aegis of the secretary of war, Henry Knox, who, knowing little about ships, consulted with advisers, prominent among whom was his friend John Wharton of Philadelphia. Wharton owned a shipyard together with his cousin Joshua Humphreys.

According to Howard I. Chapelle, in his definitive work *History of the American Sailing Navy,* the question of who actually designed these frigates is impossible to determine. Chapelle examined all known records, and concluded that it was the work of three people: Humphreys, Josiah Fox, and William Doughty. Of the three, however, Fox, an Englishman who came to Philadelphia to visit relatives and look at American timber, was the only professional naval draughtsman. He and Humphreys got on well and no doubt compared notes. So, in all likelihood, Fox was the concept man, Humphreys the engineer, and Doughty the detail man.

Of more importance, what about these designs? Was there anything new? The answer is yes. They definitely followed the English tradition but were at least twenty feet longer than a Royal Navy 44-gun frigate and slightly beamier. Being of longer water line, they were faster. Having one main gun deck they had less weight topside. This together with deeper draught enabled them to carry more sail. Probably their sail area to wetted surface ratio was higher, because they were demonstrably faster in light air. The *Constitution,* as will be seen, led a charmed life, but apart from her talented officers and skippers, the basic reason was in her design.

While the country was preparing for action with the Algerians and other "free booters," suddenly Europe erupted in another war, and this time France, under the Directory, became an anti-American predator. The French Revolution had its sympathizers in the States but certainly not in the Federalist Party, who for the most part represented the population that was benefiting from trade with Great Britain. In any case, the hostility of French ships became so notorious that in April, 1798, a Navy Department was formally established and Benjamin Stoddert was appointed secretary. The first three frigates, *United States, Constellation,* and *Constitution,* went down the ways in the previous year, and in 1798 several more ships were added to the authorization.

In May of 1798, the President was empowered to order the seizure of any French ships which threatened the commerce of the United States, and finally the old alliance with France was nullified.

The honour of the first capture under the new government and the new Navy went to Captain Stephen Decatur Sr., a Philadelphian. With the 20-gun ship *Delaware,* he overhauled a French privateer *Le Croyable,* which was condemned and converted to the United States Navy. Her name was changed to *Retaliation* and her command was given to Lieutenant William Bainbridge. This was not the last capture and renaming of this unlucky vessel.

Meanwhile the *United States* put to sea in the command of old Captain Barry, the *Constitution* in command of Nicholson, and the *Constellation* in command of Truxtun.

The squadron under Barry included the *Constitution* and eight smaller vessels, one of which, the *Pickering,* was commanded by Lieutenant Commander Preble. Several privateers were captured by this squadron and sent home. The second squadron consisted of the *Constellation, Baltimore, Richmond, Norfolk,* and *Virginia,* and their rendezvous was at St. Kitts in the West Indies. A third squadron, including the *Delaware,* cruised in Cuban waters and took a number of prizes.

The most important engagement of the war was fought by Commodore Truxtun in the *Constellation.* She was cruising downwind near Nevis in February 1799, when suddenly she sighted a man-of-war under full canvas, which, after displaying false colors, turned out to be the French 40-gun frigate *L'Insurgente,* Captain Barreault. After a torrid action lasting an hour, *L'Insurgente* struck her colors.

Truxtun put his first lieutenant Mr. Rodgers and Midshipman Porter and eleven men aboard the enemy vessel to take charge. Shortly thereafter winds of gale force struck and separated the two vessels. However, due to the skill and daring of these two officers, the prize was maneuvered in three days to St. Kitts where she found the *Constellation* already anchored.

One year later Truxtun was cruising near Guadaloupe and came upon

Plate 20 *Constellation and L'Insurgent — The Chase*

the French 52-gun frigate *Vengeance,* Captain Pitot. These two vessels went hard at it, at close quarters, for five hours, the Frenchman getting the worst of it. The enemy tactic was to shoot away the rigging, and at that she was quite successful indeed, carrying away the *Constellation*'s mainmast. At night the ships separated and the *Constellation* could not find her foe the next day. The Frenchman finally made it to Curaçao and reported her high casualties. Inasmuch as the *Constellation* was lighter in armament, it was regarded as another humiliating defeat for the Directory, which was undoubtedly suffering from a lack of good officers, having sent many of the best to the guillotine.

Peace was finally negotiated and signed early in the new year of 1801, when, in fact, the Republicans came into power. Since the latter abhorred the taxes necessary to support the marine, and basically sympathized with the French, the change in political parties virtually put an end to the conflict.

Plate 20 No. 31

Constellation & L'Insurgent — the Chase

Painted & Engraved by E. Savage.

Philada. Published by E. Savage May 20th. 1799

Aquatint. 20⅛″ by 13⅞″. Black and white.
Stauffer 2758. Grolier 15. Olds 94.

This is the first of a pair of aquatints by Savage and in fact the first aquatint done in America. Savage, who was born in Massachusetts, did this and his other works in Philadelphia. He wrote to President Washington in 1799 to advise him of this engraving on copper, a specimen of which he was holding for him.

Of the utmost rarity and importance. Only three other sets of these prints are known. One is in the New-York Historical Society, one in the Worcester Art Museum, and one in the possession of the Hollingsworth family of Boston. This set came from the Graves collection, sold at Kennedy's in 1959 to J. William Middendorf II, now Ambassador to the Netherlands. The latter sold this set to the writer in 1970. Margins are full and both prints are in mint condition.

Plate 21

No. 32

Action between the Constellation and L'Insurgent,—On the 9th. Febuary 1799,—Off the island of St. Christophers, when after an hard fought battle of one hour and a quarter the Frigate of the Directory yielded to superior skill and bravery. Killed on board L'Insurgent 29. Wounded 46. Constellation 1 killed. 3 Wounded.

Force of the Constellation	*Guns 36*
	Men 310
Force of the Insurgent	*40 . . . . Guns*
	18 . . . . Brass Swivels
	409 . . . . Men

Painted & Engraved by E. Savage.

Philada. Published by E. Savage May 20. 1799.

Aquatint. 20 1/6″ by 12 9/16″. Black and white.
Stauffer 2757. Grolier 16. Olds 95.

No. 33

Truxton's Victory

Engagement between the United States Frigate Constellation of 36 Guns, commanded by Capt. Truxton, and L'Insurgente French Frigate of 40 Guns, Capt. Bureaut, Feby. 9th., 1799.

Published and Sold by E. Pember and S. Luzerder, Philadelphia.

Line engraving. 10¾″ by 8⅛″. Colored by hand. Undated.
Fielding 1925. Grolier 17. Olds 96.

Very rare. This is a rather crude piece of work artistically and technically. Both captains' names are misspelled. On the reverse side of this print is an engraving of George Washington on his death bed, attended by Doctors Craik and Brown. As a point of interest, John Paul Jones' father worked as gardener for the Craik family in Scotland. Though undated, the print must have been issued close to the time of Washington's death, 14 December, 1799.

Plate 22

No. 34

A View of the American Frigate, Constellation, capturing the French National Frigate, L'Insurgente, within sight of Basseterre Feby. 9th. 1799. The Ships commenced a running fight near Nevis, and afterwards continued in

Plate 21 *Action between Constellation and L'Insurgent*

Plate 22 *Constellation Capturing L'Insurgente*

close Action for three quarters of an hour, when the French Frigate was compelled to strike her Colours to the Victorious Americans.

L'Insurgente 44 Guns 78 Men Killed and Wounded. Constellation 44 Guns Capn. Truxton 1 Man Killed 2 Wounded.

Publish'd Octr. 1st. 1800, by John Fairburn, 146, Minories, London.

Stipple and line engraving. 13½" by 8⅞". Artist and engraver unnamed. Black and white.

Olds 98, Grolier 18—except not colored.

Very rare. The armament stated above for both ships is in error and Truxtun's name is misspelled. Impressions of this engraving in the Olds collection and Franklin D. Roosevelt collection are colored by hand. It is a companion to the following print of the engagement between the *Planter* and a French privateer.

Plate 23 No. 35

A View of the American Merchant Ship Planter, beating off a French National Privateer of 22 Guns July 10th. 1799. The Ships fought for two Glasses and a half, when the French Privateer sheered off to repair damages, and in one Glass return'd with his Bloody Flag hoisted, with intention to Board, but was repulsed with great Slaughter—The Action lasted five Glasses and a half, when the Privateer was completely Beat off.

Planter, Captn. John Watts 18 Guns & 43 Men out of which 4 was Killed and 8 Wounded.

Publish'd Octr. 1st. 1800, by John Fairburn, 146, Minories, London.

Aquatint. 13¾" by 9". Hand colored. Artist and engraver unnamed.

Grolier 197. The Olds impression was black and white. Very rare in either state.

Plate 24 No. 36

Preparation for WAR to defend Commerce. The Swedish Church Southwark with the building of the FRIGATE PHILADELPHIA.

Drawn Engraved & Published by W. Birch & Son.

Sold by R. Campbell & Co. No. 30 Chesnut Street Philada. 1800.

Line engraving. 11 9/16" by 9 3/16". Colored by hand. First state.

Stauffer 170. Grolier 209. Olds 375.

Plate 23 *Merchant Ship Planter Beating Off a French Privateer*

Plate 24 *Preparation for War to Defend Commerce*

This print is one of a set of twenty-eight plates that appeared as a handsome book in 1800. The subscribers' list included President Thomas Jefferson and many prominent Philadelphians. The writer owned one copy of this book entitled *The City of Philadelphia in the State of Pennsylvania North America,* but it was sold to Paul Mellon of Upperville, Virginia.

An interesting aspect of this view is that in the foreground is a close-up picture of the inboard part of Wharton and Humphrey's Shipyard. In fact the prominent-looking man in the center with the tri-cornered hat is supposed to be Joshua Humphreys, personally supervising the work.

Chapter V

TO THE SHORES OF TRIPOLI

Quasi or not, the War with France, which was limited entirely to the sea, was the cause for the permanent establishment of the United States Navy. Naval actions in the Revolution were only part of a colonial revolt. The first real international test was against the French, and the American side came through victorious.

On the conclusion of this war and the reestablishment of friendly relations with France, for whom the Republicans had always displayed empathy, one might have anticipated a drastic reduction in the naval service. Surely this would have been the case, had it not been for the reappearance of the pirates of Barbary and their outrageous demands. Making matters worse was the manner of settlement of the Algerian crisis, wherein America had simply bought the peace by the gift of a frigate and the on-going payment of tribute to the Dey of Algiers. As has happened so often in history, such a settlement may cut two ways. Indeed, American generosity to the Dey had not escaped the attention of the potentates in other North African principalities. In particular, the corsairs of Tripoli were especially interested in an arrangement for themselves which would match that of Algiers.

The Bashaw of Tripoli, one Jussuf Caramalli, had come to power by deposing his brother. Since the United States had given the Dey of Algiers a frigate, the Bashaw demanded at least that much in money to dissuade him from preying on American merchantmen. The extraordinary demands were ignored, and on 14 May, 1801, the flag at the American consulate was cut down and war was declared against the United States.

The first squadron to be sent against the Tripolitan pirates was that of Commodore Richard Dale, which consisted of the *President, Philadelphia, Essex,* and *Enterprise,* and his orders were to show the flag, much as the Sixth Fleet has done so often in modern times. Operations consisted chiefly of blockading the port of Tripoli.

While the individual ship exploits are most interesting, the major significance of this four-year war was the training of officers and men that the war afforded. Nearly all the famous captains of the War of 1812 had their real training in the Mediterranean, mostly under Commodore Edward Preble. Therefore, had it not been for the pirate menace, the War of 1812 would surely have ended in a recapture of her colonies by Great Britain.

It is curious that the lot of subduing the pirates fell to the Americans. At various times a state of war existed between Tripoli and European countries, including Sweden and some of the Italian States. However, it was the American Navy that did the fighting. Rome gave the United States credit for her service to Christendom, but the Pope provided no frigates.

When, on blockade duty, the frigate *Philadelphia* ran aground in the outer harbor of Tripoli, the seamanship of Captain William Bainbridge might have been questioned. Even worse, the latter's surrender, almost without firing a gun, was hardly characteristic of Preble's officers, especially as it contrasts with the behavior later of Decatur, Somers, and the other daring men who were willing to sacrifice their lives. (Bainbridge was involved in the only surrender to the French, when the *Retaliation*, ex *Le Croyable*, was taken near Guadaloupe in the Quasi-War.) When officers like Captain Charles Morris were dismissed from the naval service, one can only wonder about the charmed life of Bainbridge. The loss of the *Philadelphia*, even though she drew 18 feet and was sailing near uncharted reefs, must have been considered a major catastrophe.

After Bainbridge and his crew were jailed in Tripoli, the American blockade continued and Preble stepped up his demonstrations, which included Decatur's famous and successful raid to destroy the *Philadelphia*, as well as many attacks on shore positions. Later a motley land force was assembled under the Bashaw's ousted brother, together with a detachment of United States Marines, and the town of Derne was captured. At this point, with Preble threatening the city from the sea and hostile movements on land, the Bashaw finally agreed to negotiate a settlement. The result of this was the release of Bainbridge and all the American seamen in custody and an end to the war, at least for the time being.

No. 37

Capt. Sterrett in the Schr. Enterprise paying tribute to Tripoli, August 1801.

M. Corne, p.

Line engraving. 6 11/16″ by 3⅜″. Black and white. Engraver and publisher unnamed. Undated.

Fielding 1903. Grolier 19. Olds 99.

Plate 25 *The Constitution Frigate*

Plate 26 *Frigate Philadelphia on the Rocks*

Plate 25 No. 38

The Constitution Frigate

Mixed method, line engraving plus aquatint. 13¾″ by 10¼″. Colored by hand. Artist and engraver unnamed. Undated. Circa 1797-1805.

Extremely rare. Not in Olds, Grolier, Stauffer, or Fielding. Only two other known impressions. One is at Peabody Museum; the other is now owned by Childs Gallery, having been purchased from the collection of the Hollingsworth family.

The origin of this print is a mystery. The only clue the writer offers is that the engraving resembles one of the frigate *United States*, also bare of lettering, by T. Clarke of Philadelphia. Clarke was working in Philadelphia between 1797 and 1800. He was born in England and committed suicide somewhere in the Southern states. The Clarke print, now in the Library of Congress collection, was engraved for *American Universal Magazine*, a publication which lasted a year and a half.

Another curious aspect of this print is that there is almost no resemblance to the *Constitution* as she looked in 1812. It shows only fourteen gun ports unevenly spaced, whereas the *Constitution* had sixteen gun ports per side, evenly spaced on her gun deck, and ports for eight more per side on her main deck. This suggests that it was done at an early date from the artist's or engraver's concept of what she would look like finished.

Close examination shows some lettering within the plate on the right side but nothing intelligible. The mixed method also suggests an early effort.

Plate 26 No. 39

The U.S. Frigate Philadelphia On The Rocks Off Tripoli. Oct. 31st. 1801.

P.S. Duval, Lith. Phila. On Stone by E. J. Pinkerton

Lithograph. 10¾″ by 7¼″. Colored by hand. Undated, first state.

Grolier 21. Olds 101. Date of action incorrect. Year should have been 1803.

On the night of 16 February, 1804, Lt. Stephen Decatur, Jr., with a party of volunteers on the ketch *Intrepid* boarded and burned the *Philadelphia* while she was at anchor under the guns of the Bashaw's castle. Decatur was an instant national hero and was promoted to captain.

Plate 27

No. 40

The burning of the American Fregate the Philadelphia in the Harbour of Tripoli happily executed by the valiant Cap: Decatur to whom this Plate is respectfully dedicated by his Obedient Servant John B. Guerrazzi.

Sold in Leghorn 1805.

Line engraving. 15½″ by 11⅜″. Black and white.
Grolier 24. Olds 104.

No. 41

Stranding and Capture of the Philadelphia.

Etched by Jos. F. Sabin from a drawing by Captain Hoff.

Etching. 7⅜″ by 4⅜″. Black and white. Publisher unnamed and undated.
Olds 106.

Plate 28

No. 42

The attack made on Tripoli on the 3d. August 1804. by the American Squadron under Commodore Edward Preble to whom this Plate is respectfully dedicated by his Obedient Servant John B. Guerrazzi.

1. Constitution Frigate 2. Sirion 3. Arges 4. Enterprise 5. Notlas 6. Vixen

Sold in Leghorn 1805.

Line engraving. 15¾″ by 11⅝″. Sepia. First state.
Grolier 26. Olds 107.

Plate 29

No. 43

Blowing Up of the Fire Ship Intrepid commanded by Capt. Somers in the Harbour of Tripoli on the night of the 4th. Sepr. 1804.

Before the Intrepid had gained her Distined situation she was suddenly boarded by 100 Tripolines, when the Gallant Somers and Heroes of his Party (Lieuts. Wadsworth and Israel and 10 Men.) observed themselves surrounded by 3 Gun-boats, and no prospect of Escape, determined at once to prefer Death and the Destruction of the Enemy, to Captivity & a torturing Slavery, put a Match to train leading directly to the Magazine, which at once blew the whole into the Air.

Plate 27 *The Burning of the Philadelphia*

Plate 28 *Attack on Tripoli*

Plate 29 *Blowing Up of the Fire Ship Intrepid*

Plate 30 *U. S. Frigate President*

Line engraving. 14″ by 9⅞″. Colored by hand. Undated. Artist, engraver, and publisher unnamed.

Grolier 29. Olds 112.

No. 43-A Same as above, except black and white.

In an effort to destroy the Tripolitan ships in the harbor of Tripoli, Richard Somers and a crew of volunteers took the *Intrepid,* loaded with combustibles, into the harbor at night. They were discovered prematurely, and all that is known is that the magazine exploded. It is pure conjecture that it was done deliberately. All on board lost their lives, which suggests an accident.

No. 44

Barque Genoise
Courant vent barque

Corvette des Etats-Unis D' Amérique
En panne, pour recevoir un Pilote à bord

Dessinées et Gravées par Baujean

Line engraving. 18 7/16″ by 11⅝″. Black and white. Undated. Believed to be the corvette *John Adams* on station in the Mediterranean.

Not in Olds, Stauffer, or Grolier. This print came from the Havemeyer collection.

Plate 30

No. 45

La Fregate des Etats-unis d'Amerique, le President, venant d'appareiller, avec des ris dans les Huniers.

Dessiné et Gravé par Baugean.

Line engraving. 7″ by 5″. Colored by hand. Not dated. Figure 13 in upper right corner.

Olds 381.

Judging from the background, i.e., the lateen rigged felucca, the shoreline, and the appearance of a squadron, the writer judges this print to depict the *President* under command of Commodore Barron arriving in the Mediterranean to relieve Commodore Preble. A translation of the inscription is "The United States Frigate President getting underway with a reef in her topsails."

Chapter VI

WAR OF 1812

Though relatively obscure in the panoply of history and probably even avoidable had cooler heads prevailed, the War of 1812 was by all odds the high water mark of the glory of the American sailing Navy. Its victories in single ship actions, its organization, its fleet actions on the Lakes, the national resolve against Britannia, all these combined to give the American nation the spirit of a winner. This was vital in the early years of the country. American prestige became established internationally and once and for all the question of independence was settled.

The war might not have been fought and certainly would not have been won had not Britain been engaged in a desperate life or death struggle against Napoleon from 1803 through 1814. One is apt to forget that this war with Britain was only part of the Napoleonic scenario. In the contest between England and Europe, the United States was neutral, but as such its commerce was subject to the predatory policies of the combatants. From time to time it fell victim to blockader and blockaded. In the first instance its commerce suffered from the Royal Navy's implementation of Orders in Council, which in effect instructed the Navy to search and seize any cargo suspected of being destined for the enemy. This was almost national piracy and had no justification in international law. But law or no law, Britain was involved in total war and these tactics were as blunt as those of the Allies in both World Wars, when anyone not a friend was assumed an enemy. Simply stated, the end justified the means. She had one hundred fifty years of maritime commerce behind her, and her statesmen recognized the importance of her marine, and unlike the youthful United States, she did everything to nurture it. She had learned this lesson from the Anglo-Dutch Wars, which gave birth to the Navigation Acts, restricting trade to British bottoms. Great Britain was a little island, and her leaders knew she had to rule the waves around it.

In addition to search and seizure of cargoes, Britain went even further. She considered it her inalienable right to search for and seize any seaman suspected of British birth. The impressment of seamen grew to outlandish proportions. By 1812, 6,000 cases of impressment were reported to Washington, and even Lord Castlereagh admitted in Parliament that the Royal Navy had 3,300 Americans in service. This intolerable practice, more than any other single cause, was the igniting factor in the United States' declaration of war.

Another source of pressure for war was the restlessness on the Western frontier spurred by Britain's furtive support of the Indians. Many of the Westerners were called "war hawks," and their concern was fear of a British-Canadian takeover. Paradoxically, the Republican (now the Democratic) Party of Jefferson and Madison, which derived much of its support from the West and South, had been the chief opponent of international entanglements and was tenaciously opposed to appropriations for the Navy. Its high priest was Representative Albert Gallatin of Pennsylvania, whose counsel carried weight with Jefferson. To Gallatin the Navy was a luxury at best. When Madison was elected president in 1803, Gallatin was appointed secretary of the treasury. During these years, about all the administration allowed was a second rate gunboat navy. Thus, the most effective means for protecting American rights, a combat-ready navy, was kept impotent by the very politicians who elected to wage war.

While the insults and outrages on the part of the British persisted, the mood of the country gradually shifted to a preference for war. Just at this point, had the leaders held off, they might have found Britain willing to back down and be reasonable. In fact, in Britain there was a strong pro-American sentiment among a faction that held it was unwise policy to nettle the United States. In the last few weeks while war was being considered by America, Britain actually rescinded her Orders in Council. She finally realized her high seas policies had gone too far, but communications being what they were, the United States proceeded to declare war before news of any change had arrived.

The chronology of events leading to the war and the war itself consisted of many separate and distinct actions. Probably the first affair, which alarmed everyone but Congress, was the engagement between the *Chesapeake* and *Leopard* in June 1807. HMS *Leopard* was part of Admiral Berkeley's North American squadron, based at Halifax. In the previous year during a hurricane in the West Indies two French men-of-war had escaped from a British squadron and sought refuge in Chesapeake Bay. Admiral Berkeley sent a force to guard the entrance of the Chesapeake and to capture the French ships when they put to sea. This blockade lasted the whole winter, and during periods ashore in Norfolk when the ships on this station were in for fresh water, victuals, and repairs, the opportunities for seamen to jump ship were just too tempting. Several deserters joined

American ships which were not at war but needed crews.

One such ship, the *Chesapeake,* flying the broad pennant of Commodore James Barron, had fitted out first at Washington Navy Yard, then at Norfolk. At the time she was ordered to sea, the *Chesapeake* was in a most unprepared state. She had had no gunnery practice, and furthermore, she carried diplomats and their families bound for the Mediterranean. In short, she was totally unfit for battle. In this state she was overtaken by HMS *Leopard,* one of the British squadron on station. The latter's orders were to recover seamen known to have been deserters. Commodore Barron refused to give up anyone, and the *Leopard* opened fire on her. All hands on the *Chesapeake* were in total confusion and the ship never got off a broadside. Barron ordered the colors struck, and, after the British seized the men they sought, they permitted the *Chesapeake* to limp back to Norfolk and report her fate. Barron was later courtmartialed and dismissed from the naval service for five years. More importantly, this action set off a long series of diplomatic protests, charges and countercharges which, together with other incidents, consumed the better part of four years.

During the period of President Madison's administration events continued to suggest a collision course with England. Still, the politicians voted for coastal defense by a gunboat navy. By 1809, the frigates *United States, President,* and *Essex* and corvette *John Adams* were put into commission along with the *Constitution,* which was never decommissioned. At the start of war in 1812 the United States had 17 ships, Britain 1,048. The United States had 15,300 tons, Britain 860,990 tons. The United States had 442 guns and 5,000 men and Britain 27,800 guns and 150,000 men. Even on the North American station alone, from Halifax to Bermuda and the West Indies, Britain had seven times the armament of the entire American Navy. Besides this she had navy yards and dry docks, whereas the United States had allowed the few facilities that had existed to rot in disuse. This was the relative situation when war was finally declared.

EVENTS OF THE WAR

One of the many incidents preceding the declaration of war was that of the *President-Little Belt* encounter. Commodore John Rodgers, whose broad pennant flew at the truck of the USS *President,* was at home in

Plate 31 *The Little Belt and President*

Plate 32 *The President and Little Belt*

Havre de Grace, Maryland. Suddenly he got word from Washington that HMS *Guerriere* was cruising off the coast south of New York and had actually taken a United States citizen off a privateer bound from Portland to New York. He dashed forthwith down to his gig and was rowed at flank speed to Annapolis, where the USS *President* was at anchor off Fort Severn. On 12 May, 1811, the *President* got under way down the bay and on 16 May, after she had passed the Capes into the Atlantic, a strange sail was sighted to the eastward.

From the looks of her topsails she was mistaken for *Guerriere,* but later proved to be the 22-gun ship *Little Belt,* Captain Arthur Butt Bingham. Rodgers wasted no time getting alongside and hailing. *Little Belt* was said to have fired first; at least all the Americans so testified later. At any rate, the 44-gun *President* poured a few broadsides into the smaller brig, killed eleven and wounded seventy-two. As war had not been declared, the *President* withheld further firing and came alongside to offer assistance to the badly damaged *Little Belt.* It was declined, and the two ships proceeded on their way. This very uneven contest resulted in a "friendly" Court of Inquiry at which the presiding officer was Stephen Decatur, a hawk of the first degree. Rodgers was cleared with praise for his conduct.

Plate 31 No. 46

The Little Belt, Sloop of War, Captn. Bingham nobly supporting the Honor of the British Flag, against the President United States Frigate, Commodore Rogers, May 15th. 1811

Wm. Elmes delt. Wm. Elmes sculpt.

Pubd. & Sold Octr. 25 1811, by Edwd. Orme, Printseller to his Majesty & Royal Family, Engraver & Publisher, Bond St. corner of Brook St. London.

Aquatint. 19½" by 14 9/16". Colored by hand.
Grolier 30. Olds 113.

Plate 32 No. 47

To the Right Honorable Charles Philip Yorke, First Lord of the Admiralty, This Print elucidating the extreme disproportion of Force between the American Frigate President Commodore Rodgers, and His Majesty's Sloop the Little Belt Arthur Butt Bingham Esquire Commander, and representing the situation of both Ships in the morning after the Action of the 11 May 1811, is respectfully inscribed by his obliged Servant Josh. Cartwright.

Drawn by J. Cartwright. Engraved by J. Hassell.

London, Pub. 1 Dec. 1811 by J. Hassell, N°. 11 Clements Inn, & J. Cartwright, 39, Arundel Street, Strand.

Description of armament and crew of each ship below the view.
Aquatint. 20¼" by 13⅞". Colored by hand. Date in the caption incorrect.
Grolier 31. Olds 114.

No. 48

The American Frigate PRESIDENT Commodore Rogers, engaging the little Belt Captn. Bingham

Printed & Published by Langley & Belch, N°. 173 High St. Borough London

Mixed method, stipple and line engraving. 7⅛" by 4⅞". Black and white. Artist and engraver not named. Undated. Rodgers' name is misspelled and so is Little Belt.
Grolier 32. Not in Olds. Ex Havemeyer collection.

Plate 33

No. 49

The Capture of the Gipsey Schooner New York on the 30th. of April 1812, by H. M. Ships Hermese and Bélle Poule In the Middle of the Atlantic Ocean after a Chase of three days and nights; she was bound from New York to Bordeaux with a Cargo Value 50,000 L, a Crew of Eighty Men, and supposed to be a Privateer, being fully armed and Equiped.

Painted by W.J. Huggins, Marine Painter to His Majesty, & Published by Him, at 105, Leadenhall Street, Septr. 10th. 1834. Engraved by Rosenberg.

Aquatint. 17⅛" by 10¾". Colored by hand.
Very rare first state of this print. Not in Grolier. Not in Olds. Note misspelling of Hermes.

No. 50

The Capture of the Gipsey Schooner of New York on the 30th. of April 1812, by H. M. Ships Hermes and Belle Poule In the Middle of the Atlantic Ocean, after a Chase of three days and nights; she was bound from New York to Bordeaux with a Cargo Value 50,000 L. The Schooner was a most superb Vessel of 300 Tons burthen carried Ten 18lb. Carronades and one long 18 pound swivel between her main & foremast with a complement of 80 Men & 2 Ferocious Dogs. She had twice surrender'd to the Hermes previous to falling in with the Belle Poule & endeavoured to effect her es-

Plate 33 *Capture of the Gipsey Schooner New York*

cape each time by hauling off on a different tack, while the ship was in the act of taking in sail & rounding to. The Crew of the American made a desperate effort to regain possession of their Vessel after being boarded by the boats of the Hermes by 20 Armed Men and the Two Dogs suddenly assailing them, which after a severe struggle were overpowered.

Painted by W. J. Huggins, Marine Painter to His Majesty for Charles Augustus Manning, Esqre. Portland Castle, Dorsetshire, from a Design by Captn. Philip Browne, R.N. Commander of H.M.S. Hermes. Engraved by C. Rosenberg.

Aquatint. 17″ by 10¾″. Colored by hand. Not dated. While the rendition of this print, which Olds calls second state, is the same as the preceding, it bears little resemblance in the inscription. The spelling of Hermes is corrected.
Grolier 199. Olds 360.

This privateer action was one of many that occurred during the period and is thus illustrative of one of the essential causes of the war. In fairness, however, it should be said that she was bound for Bordeaux and therefore a blockade runner.

No. 51

Belvidera & President

J. A. Wright sc.

Lithograph after drawing by John Allan Wright. Vignette 8⅞″ by 4¼″. Hand colored.
Olds 116, except colored.

This encounter occurred five days after declaration of war when the frigate *President*, Commodore Rodgers, was cruising off New York with the commodore's squadron. *Belvidera* escaped after heaving most of her guns overboard.

No. 52

Constitution's Escape from the British Squadron after a chase of sixty hours.

M. Corne p. W. Hoogland Sc.

Engraved For The Naval Monument (at top)

Entered according to Act of Congress Nov. 25, 1815 by A. Bowen.

Line engraving. 7¾″ by 3 15/16″. Colored by hand.
Stauffer 1436. Grolier 35. Olds 119a.

This event in some ways attests to the skill of Captain Isaac Hull better even than his later famous engagement with the *Guerriere,* because he was able to escape from a vastly superior force by tremendous effort. He moved the frigate by kedging, by towing with ship's boats, and finally by picking up light zephyrs of air and outsailing his adversaries.

The *Constitution* had come out of Chesapeake Bay seeking the *Guerriere,* but instead she fell into the whole squadron of which the *Guerriere* was just one part.

CONSTITUTION—GUERRIERE
19 AUGUST, 1812

Captain Isaac Hull, although he had some questionable business dealings in his earlier days, was perhaps the most respected and most competent American naval captain of the times. He did not have the charisma and daring of Decatur, nor the fleet command capability of Preble, nor even the technical competence of Truxtun, but he was without peer as a captain, especially to the men.

When he first got the *Constitution* to sea, he ran smack into the squadron previously mentioned. After successfully eluding the enemy, Hull put into Boston briefly for provisions. Then he set sail eastward. On the night of 18 August, 1812, he overtook an American privateer, the *Decatur,* who warned him of the whereabouts of a British frigate further to the east. The next day he caught up with the *Guerriere,* Captain James R. Dacres, and after a spirited single ship action of forty minutes, the *Guerriere* surrendered. The latter had to be blown up and sunk, and Hull took the enemy's officers and crew to Boston in triumph. This was the first ship victory of the war and as such the most famous. Hull was an instant hero, and Boston went wild over him, as did the rest of the country.

Plate 34 *Engagement between the Constitution and Guerriere*

Plate 34

No. 53

Engagement between the U.S. Frigate Constitution Capt. Hull rating 44 Guns & the British Frigate Guerriere Capt. Dacres rated 38 Guns; August 19th. 1812; which terminated in the complete destruction of the Enemy's Ship after a close Action of 30 minutes Loss of the British 15 killed 62 wounded 24 missing ——— American loss 7 killed 7 wounded.

Designed by T. Birch. F. Kearney Aquatint.

Aquatint. Colored by hand. Undated. No publisher listed.

This print, in mint condition, is of the utmost rarity, perhaps the rarest in the collection. Rudolf G. Wunderlich in his catalogue of Kennedy Galleries, May 7-31, 1959, states that he knows of two others extant, one being Olds 123. He is incorrect in one respect; the Olds copy of the same print had a publisher's line, which clearly was added later. Thus, the writer believes this one to be first state and Mr. Olds' copy second state. Of course, it is rare in any state, not listed in Stauffer, Fielding, or Grolier. It came from the Francis P. Garvan collection via Kennedy's. Kearney was an engraver and published prints at the southwest corner of Sansom and 7th Streets in Philadelphia.

Plate 35

No. 54

This Representation Of The U.S. Frigate Constitution, Isaac Hull, Esqr. Commander, Capturing His Britannic Majesty's Frigate Guerriere, James R. Dacres Esqr. Commander; Is respectfully inscribed to Capt. Isaac Hull, his Officers and Gallant Crew; by their devoted humble Servant, James Webster. Fought August 19, 1812.

The Constitution had 7 men killed & 7 wounded. The Guerriere had 15 men killed & 63 wounded.

Painted by T. Birch, A.C.S.A. Engraved by C. Tiebout, A.C.S.A.

Entered according to Act of Congress the 18th. day of August 1813 by James Webster of State of Pennsylvania.

The subscription price of $5.00 is rubbed out. The small bust portrait of Captain Hull, face toward left, engraved by David Edwin, surrounded by flags, eagle, cannon, anchor, etc., in vignette at center of bottom margin, inscribed at top: "Veni, Vidi, Vici." Names of Barralet and Edwin below the vignette. Detailed description of the engagement.

Stipple engraving. 26⅜" by 17¾". Colored by hand.

Stauffer 3206. Grolier 36. Olds 120.

No. 55

This Portrait of Captn. Isaac Hull, of the United States Navy; also the representation of the most interesting scene during the Action, between the United States Frigate Constitution, and his Britannic Majesty's Frigate Guerriere, is most respectfully dedicated to the People of the United States, by their fellow Citizens, Freeman & Pierie.

Gilbert Stuart Esqr. Pinxit. Freeman, Excudit.

The Vignette, from an Original Drawing, under the direction of Captn. Hull.

Published at Philadelphia, & Entered according to Act of Congress, the 1st. day of February 1813, by Freeman and Pierie, of the State of Pennsylvania.

Large portrait of Hull at top. Vignette below of engagement between *Constitution* and *Guerriere.*
Mezzotint. 14¾" by 13⅜". Black and white.
First state. Olds 455.

On this rare print there is considerable disagreement among experts. First of all, no two descriptions have the same dimensions. Secondly, some confusion exists over state. Olds' view that the one published by T. Freeman alone was the first state is not supported by the writer. Middendorf claims the Freeman & Pierie publication to be first state, as does the Library of Congress. To confuse matters further, Stauffer attributes the engraving to George Graham, although giving no support to that theory.

Having both impressions of this fine print, the writer concluded that Mr. Olds is incorrect and that the Library of Congress and Ambassador Middendorf are right. The earlier strike is the one dedicated by Freeman & Pierie and the second state by T. W. Freeman alone. The telltale evidence, which shows up under twenty times magnification, is that of a change in the dedication line. Except for this discovery, all the circumstantial evidence would appear to favor the T. W. Freeman one as the older. For example, Pierie was a partner of Kearney in 1812, and Freeman advertised his upcoming print in late 1812. Furthermore, Freeman and Pierie appear as partners in the 1813 Directory of Philadelphia, but in no other year does either appear. Therefore, it would be logical to conclude that Freeman took Pierie in as a partner but did not include him on the dedication line in the first strike. On the other hand, perhaps there was a falling-out of partners and Pierie went elsewhere, after which Freeman dropped Pierie's name from the dedication line. As I have stated, microscopic examination favors the

Plate 35 *Constitution and Guerriere*

Plate 36 *Portrait of Isaac Hull*

latter circumstances, which indeed is the position of Stauffer, the Library of Congress, and Ambassador Middendorf.

The writer has a lengthy letter from Isaac Hull to Thomas Chew wherein the subject of posing for Stuart was discussed. Chew apparently arranged for the painting. In commenting on the representations of the engagement that had been submitted to him, Hull wrote Chew, "You was mistaken about the *Guerriere* being on our weather quarter—her bowsprit was over our lee quarter and rested on the boat davit the first views were correct except some little things pointed out by you."

Plate 36 No. 56

Same print as above except second state with only the name of T. Freeman on the dedication line.

Mezzotint. 14¾" by 13⅜". Colored by hand.

Olds 454. Other imps.: Brown University (state II); Boston Public Library (state II); Chicago Historical Society (state II); Connecticut Historical Society (state II); Library of Congress; New-York Historical Society (state I); New York Public Library (state II); The White House (state I); Yale University (state I).

Plate 37 No. 57

Brilliant Naval Victory, With the U. States Frigate Constitution of 44 Guns, Capn. Hull, & the English Frigate Guerriere of 38 Guns, Capn. Dacres, in which action Capn. Hull lost 7 men killed, & 7 wounded, & his B.Ms. Ship was sunk; besides her loss of 15 men killed, 62 wounded, & 24 missing; August 20, 1812. After closing, the action was 30 minus.

S. Seymour delin sculp.

Line engraving. 16⅝" by 11⅞". Colored by hand. Undated. Rare first state. This print has no publisher's line. In other respects it is the same as Fielding 1428, Grolier 38, and Olds 124, which have the following added: "Philadelphia. Published by J. Pierie & F. Kearney 1812." It appears therefore that this is a first state and that the others are second state. It came from the Havemeyer collection.

Plate 38 No. 58

Signal Naval Victory, Achieved by Capt. Hull, of the U.S. Frigate Constitution, over H. B. Majesty's Frigate Guerriere Capt. Dacres; which terminated in the total destruction of the Enemy's Ship, after a close Action of 30 Minutes.

Plate 37 *Brilliant Naval Victory*

Plate 38 *Signal Naval Victory*

Engagement took place Aug$^{t.}$ 19 1812 at 6 O'Clock P.M.

Design'd Engraved & Publish'd by W. Strickland & W. Kneass Philad$^{a.}$ 21$^{t.}$ Sept. 1812.

Statement of the armament and losses of each ship at the sides.
Line engraving. 13½" by 9¾". Colored by hand.
Stauffer 1660. Grolier 41. Olds 125.

Plate 39

No. 59

Engagement between the U.S. Frigate Constitution Capt$^{n.}$ Isaac Hull, & the British Frigate Guerriere, Capt$^{n.}$ James R. Dacres, Thursday 19$^{th.}$ August 1812.

There are extracts from Captain Hull's letters describing the engagement, and a statement of the armament and losses of each ship is set forth at the sides of the title.

Published Oct$^{r.}$ 1$^{st.}$ 1812, by B. Tanner N$^{o.}$ 74 South 8$^{th.}$ S$^{t.}$ Philadelphia.

Line engraving. 14 15/16" by 11". Colored by hand. Engraved by Tanner after Barralet. First state.
Fielding 1544. Grolier 39. Olds 126.

Plate 40

No. 60

Explosion of the British Frigate, Guerriere, James R. Dacres, Esq$^{r.}$ Capt$^{n.}$ and Rescue of the Prisoners, &c. the day after her Capture by the U.S. Frigate Constitution Isaac Hull Esq$^{r.}$ Comm$^{r.}$ Friday 20$^{th.}$ August 1812.

J. J. Barralet Del$^{t.}$ B. Tanner Sculp$^{t.}$

Published Nov$^{r.}$ 10$^{th.}$ 1812 by B. Tanner N$^{o.}$ 74 South 8$^{th.}$ S$^{t.}$ Phil$^{a.}$

There are extracts from Captain Hull's letters describing the incident which are set forth at the sides of the title.
Line engraving, 15" by 11⅛". Colored by hand. The second of a pair by Tanner after Barralet. First state.
Fielding 1545. Grolier 40. Olds 127.

Plate 41

No. 61

La Constitution Et La Guerrière + The Constitution and the Guerriere.

Chez lordereau Rue S$^{t.}$ Jacques, N$^{o.}$ 59, à Paris. Lith. par Betremieux. r. des Vinaigriers N$^{o.}$ 25. Déposé.

Plate 39 *Engagement of Constitution and Guerriere*

Plate 40 *Explosion of the Guerriere*

Lithograph. 25½" by 18¾". Colored by hand. Undated.
Grolier 57. Olds 131. Rare.

Plate 42 No. 62

The U.S. frigate Constitution Commanded by Isaac Hull, Esqr. Captured his B. M. frigate Guerriere Capt. Dacres in 30 Minutes On the 19th. of August 1812.

Pubd. by Chs. D. Veechio, 136 Broad Way.

Stipple engraving. 9⅜" by 6⅛". Colored by hand. Undated.
This print was Grolier 43, being lent to the Grolier Show by the late Henry O. Havemeyer, from whose estate it was purchased by the writer. Olds 128. Both Olds and Grolier assert this is second state. A black and white version of this same print was also obtained in the same sale and given to the Philadelphia Maritime Museum.

Plate 43 No. 63

Prise de la frégate anglaise la Guerrière, par la frégate américaine la Constitution. The English frigate Warrior Captur'd By the american frigate Constitution.

"No. 4" in right corner of upper margin.

Dessiné par Montardier du Havre. Gravé par Baugean

A Paris, chez Jean, rue St. Jean de Beauvais. No. 10

Line engraving. 16⅞" by 11¼". Colored by hand. Undated. Believed to be 1814. First state. Both Olds and Grolier copies not colored. This is the fourth in a series by Baugean after Montardier, all of 1812 actions.
Olds 130. Grolier 49.

No. 64

Prise d'un Vaisseau Anglais par un Vaisseau Américain.

Gravé par Debucourt.

Line engraving. 7 7/16" by 4 15/16". Black and white. Undated.
Olds 132.

Plate 41 *The Constitution and the Guerriere*

Plate 42 *The Constitution Capturing His B.M. Frigate Guerriere*

Plate 43 *Capture of the Guerriere*

Plate 44

No. 65

LA FRÉGATE AMÉRICAINE La Constitution Prenant à L'abordage, La Frégate Anglaise, La Guèrriere (Après 30 minutes de Combat, le 19 Aout 1812.)

Stradonwort Pinx. Valnest sculp.

A Paris chez Basset Rue S. Jacques No. 64 Déposé

Aquatint. 18⅛" by 12⅞". Colored by hand. Undated.
Grolier 50. Olds 133.

No. 66

The Constitution and Guerriere. Fought, August 19, 1812.

The Guerriere had 15 men killed & 63 wounded. The Constitution had 7 men killed & 7 wounded.

Lith. & Pub. by N. Currier, 2 Spruce St. N.Y.

Lithograph. 12 7/16" by 8 3/16". Colored by hand. Undated.
H. T. Peters 1124. Olds 139.

Plate 45

No. 67

Engagement between the American Frigate The Constitution, and the English Frigate The Guerriere, surrendered after having been entirely disabled. Combat entre la Frégate Américaine la Constitution, et la Frégate Anglaise la Guerriere, qui s'est rendue après avoir été entièrement désemparée. Dedicated to the Deffenders of the Seas.

Baugean del. Jazet sculp.

Déposé A Paris chez Osterwald l'ainé Editeur, Rue de la Parcheminerie No. 2.

Aquatint. 16½" by 11⅜". Colored by hand. Undated. Rare.
Grolier 51. Not in Olds. This copy came from the Hicks collection.

* * *

Although this is basically a collection of prints, a few water color paintings are included, as they pertain to the subject matter and are a part of the writer's collection:

Plate 46 No. 68

Water color painting of *Constitution* and *Guerriere* by W.A.K. Martin.

13″ by 7¾″. Signed.

No. 69

Water color drawing of U.S. Ship *Constitution* by W.A.K. Martin with details.

15½″ by 11½″. Signed.

Plate 47 No. 70

Miniature water color of USS *Constitution* at Table Bay, Cape of Good Hope.

One of an oval pair, by the French artist Ambroise Louis Garneray (1783-1857). This is a most remarkable painting that must have been done under a magnifying glass. It has boats in the harbor in minute detail.
Diameter 3⅝″. Signed.

Garneray did a series of six oils of the War of 1812 now in the possession of Winterthur Museum. The artist went to sea at the age of 13, and in 1806 he was taken prisoner by the British. He stayed in Britain until 1814, during which time he studied aquatint. After he returned to France he was patronized by King Louis XVIII. He designed and engraved sixty-four views of the principal ports of France and forty views of foreign ports. These were published from 1821 to 1832. There are three of his paintings at the Versailles Gallery, one at the Boulogne Museum, one at Marseilles Museum, one at Nantes, one at Rochefort, one at Rochelle, and one at Rouen.

Plate 48 No. 71

Oval painting in water color of the *Wasp* and *Frolic* by Ambroise Louis Garneray.

Diameter 3½″. Companion to that of *Constitution* at Table Bay, South Africa. Signed. Harry Shaw Newman believed this painting to be that of the *Wasp* and *Frolic* and so stated in his covering letter to the author. He found this pair in Paris in the early 1950's.

* * *

No. 72

The Wasp Boarding The Frolic

M. Corne, p.   A. Bowen, sc.

Woodcut 6 11/16″ by 3¼″. Colored by hand. Undated.

Plate 44 *The American Frigate Constitution Capturing the English Frigate Guerriere*

Plate 45 *The Engagement between the Constitution and the Guerriere*

Plate 46 *Constitution and Guerriere* (watercolor)

Plate 47 *Constitution at Table Bay* (watercolor)

No. 73

Jacob Jones Esqr. of the United States Navy

Rembt. Peale Pt. D. Edwin sc.

Engraved for the Analectic Magazine

Entered according to Act of Congress.

Stipple engraving. 3 15/16″ by 3 5/16″. Colored by hand.

Plate 49

No. 74

U.S. Frigate Constitution, of 44 Guns.

Drawn by Wm. Lynn. A Bowen Sc.

Boston, Pubd. by Wm. Lynn.

Mixed method engraving, line and aquatint. 21 1/16″ by 15 15/16″. Sky and sails printed in color. Flag, pennant, and hull colored by hand. Undated. Stauffer 233. Grolier 214. Olds 379.

Since Abel Bowen was born in 1790 and became a rigger by trade, it is most probable he did this print shortly after the famous victory over the *Guerriere,* when the *Constitution* was in Boston and ship and skipper were basking in national acclaim. This was Bowen's only large engraving; most of his work was in woodcuts for book illustrations.

This is a bold and outstanding print in mint condition from the Middendorf collection. Extremely rare. Mr. Olds and Ambassador Middendorf call this a line engraving. The writer disagrees. I believe the top part of the print to be aquatint, the bottom line engraving. In any case, it is one of the outstanding items of the collection.

Other imps.: David B. Robb; Marian S. Carson; New-York Historical Society; Metropolitan Museum of Art; Museum of Fine Arts, Boston; Peabody Museum, Salem.

No. 75

U.S. Frigate Constitution.

Lith. & Pub. by N. Currier 2 Spruce St. N.Y.

Lithograph 12½″ by 8 1/16″. Colored by hand. Undated.
H. T. Peters 1121. Olds 384.

Plate 48 *The Wasp and Frolic* (watercolor)

Plate 49 *U. S. Frigate Constitution*

WASP AND FROLIC

The next single ship action in chronological order was that of the brigs *Wasp* and *Frolic* on 18 October, 1812. The *Wasp*, Captain Jacob Jones, had hardly cleared the coast on an eastward cruise to intercept shipping, when she sighted a convoy of merchantmen escorted by one sloop of size and armament comparable to the *Wasp*. She turned out to be HMS *Frolic*, and the latter immediately covered her convoy and cleared for action. At first the British vessel seemed to be getting the better of it, but at very close quarters *Frolic* hooked her bowsprit into *Wasp* and swung bow to. This enabled *Wasp* to pour in broadside after deadly broadside, while the English gunners were unable to aim at their target.

The first lieutenant, Mr. James Biddle, jumped on board with a party of men and found the enemy devastated. Biddle himself hauled the *Frolic*'s ensign down.

Shortly after Jones ordered a prize crew aboard his captive, the two vessels were overhauled by a British 74, HMS *Poictiers*, and captured without resistance. The *Wasp* and *Frolic* were then escorted to Bermuda, and exchanges and releases were arranged.

Plate 50 — No. 76

The Capture of H.B.M. Sloop of War Frolic, Capn. Whinyates, by the U.S. Sloop of War Wasp, Capn. Jab. Jones, on the 18th. of Octr. 1812, after a close Action of 43 Minutes. Soon after the Frolic Surrendered, both her Masts went by the Board: she had 6 Merchant's Ships under her Convoy.

Drawn & Engraved by F. Kearny, from a Sketch by Lieut. Claxton, of the Wasp.

Published by F. Kearny S.W. corner of Sansom & 7th. Street Phila.

Statement of armament and losses at the sides.

Aquatint. 16⅜″ by 11¾″. Colored by hand. Undated. First state.

Not in Stauffer or Grolier. Olds 148. The second state, in both Grolier and Stauffer, was published by C. P. Fessenden. There was also a third state published in Boston by Prentiss and Whitney.

Plate 51 — No. 77

Prise de la corvette anglais Forlic par la corvette américaine Wasp. The English sloop of war Forlic captur'd By the american sloop of war Wasp.

Plate 50 *Capture of the Frolic by the Wasp*

Plate 51 *The Frolic Captured by the Wasp*

Dessiné par Montardier du Havre   Gravé par Baugean

A Paris, chez Jean, Rue St. Jean de Beauvais No. 10.

Line engraving. 16⅞″ by 11⅛″. Colored by hand. Undated. One of a set of four by Baugean. First state. Later states have Frolic spelled correctly and Baugean changed to Baujean.
Grolier 63. Olds 153.

No. 78

James Biddle Esqr. Of the United States Navy

Wood, del.   Gimbrede, Sculpt.

Engraved for the Analectic Magazine

Published by M. Thomas

Stipple engraving. 3 15/16″ by 3 5/16″. Colored by hand.

No. 79

A Wasp taking a Frolick Or a Sting for Johnny Bull.

Wm. Charles Del et Sculp

Standing figure of John Bull, sword in right hand, stung through his middle by the tail of a wasp. John Bull is saying:

I've often heard of your Wasps and Hornet's but little thought such diminitive Insects could give me such a sting!!!

Poem at bottom reads:

A Wasp took a Frolick, and met Johnny Bull Who always fights best when his belly is full, The Wasp thought him hungry by his mouth open wide So his belly to fill put her Sting in his side.

Ocean and outline of two ships in the background.
Etching. Rectangle. 10⅞″ by 8⅞″. Colored by hand. Undated.
Stauffer 321. Olds 429.

Plate 52

No. 80

Johnny Bull in a Fret Oh these Wasps & Hornets! the dreadful little Insects, how they Sting! Oh woe is me! why did I disturb Their Nest!!
Pubd. at 72 Chestnut St. Phila.

Plate 52 Caricature by William Charles

Standing, stamping figure of John Bull, pursued by seven wasps and hornets. Ocean and outlines of five single-ship engagements in the background.

Etching by William Charles. Rectangle. 11″ by 9 3/16″. Colored by hand. Undated.

Stauffer 326. Olds 430.

UNITED STATES AND MACEDONIAN

Captain Stephen Decatur, Jr. was appointed to the command of one of the country's finest ships, the *United States.* At the outset she was part of Commodore Rodgers' squadron, which had singularly bad luck in finding the enemy. Decatur may not have thought it was just bad luck. In any case, he managed to get detached from Rodgers and went on a cruise to the south with only the brig *Argus* accompanying his flagship. After dispatching the *Argus* to search along the shipping lanes, Decatur fell in with HMS *Macedonian,* a frigate of similar size and armament to his own. In relatively short order it was clear that the American gunnery was superior. *Macedonian* struck, and a prize crew was put aboard in command of Lieutenant William Allen.

Both vessels then proceeded to Newport, Rhode Island, and thence down the sound through Hell Gate to New York. The dashing Decatur, already a national hero after the *Philadelphia* incident, thus became the first officer to bring a British man-of-war as prize into an American port.

That was October of 1812, and, hard as it is to believe, Congress had still not authorized any further ship construction. This hesitancy may well have stemmed from the defeatist idea that, since the French built so many ships that ended in the Royal Navy, the United States should not risk similar loss. By the close of 1812, however, national pride and confidence in the United States Navy had reached an all-time high.

Decatur's great victory, together with his sense of the dramatic—bringing his prize all the way from the Canary Islands to New York—must be regarded as a high-water mark in American naval lore.

Plate 53 No. 81

Capture of H.B.M. Frigate Macedonian, Captn. John S. Carden by the U.S. Frigate United States, Stephen Decatur Esqr. Commander. To Commodore

Plate 53 *Capture of the Macedonian by the United States*

Decatur, his Officers and Brave Crew; This Plate is Dedicated with the Greatest respect by B. Tanner.

Painted by T. Birch, P.A.   Engraved by B. Tanner.

Entered according to Act of Congress, the 13th. day of August 1813 by Benjamin Tanner of the State of Pennsylvania. Published 25th. October, 1813, by B. Tanner, Engraver, No. 74 South Eighth Street, Philadelphia.

Extracts from Decatur's Official Letter at bottom of the print. Statement of armament and losses at the right side. Small oval bust portrait of Capt. Decatur, facing toward right, in vignette at center of bottom margin, inscribed:

October 25, 1812. Free Trade and No Impressment.

Line engraving. 26″ by 18⅞″. Black and white. First state.

Not in Stauffer. Not in Olds in black and white. Not in Grolier in this state. This print came from Joseph Kindig, antique dealer of York, Pennsylvania, in its original frame.

No. 82

United States and Macedonian.

At sides:

Extract from Commodore Decatur's Official Letter: "At Sea, Octr. 30th. 1812. On the 25th. Inst. being in latitude 29 degs. N. Longitude 29 degs. 30 mins. W. we fell in with, and after an action of an hour and a half, Captured his Britannic Majesty's Ship, Macedonian commanded by Captain John Carden, and mounting 49 carriage Guns." The U. States had 5 killed and 7 wounded the Macedonian 36 K & 68 W.

Painted by T. Birch. Engraved by B. Tanner.

Published 1st. November 1814, by B. Tanner, Engraver, No. 74 South Eighth Street, Philadelphia. Entered according to Act of Congress the 13th. day of August 1813 by Benjamin Tanner of the State of Pennsylvania.

Line engraving. 24½″ by 17¼″. Black and white. This is probably third state. It has "printed by Canmeyer and Acock" on lower left side.

Plate 54

No. 83

This Representation Of the U.S. Frigate United States, Stephen Decatur Esqr. Commander, Capturing His Britannic Majesty's Frigate Macedonian, John S. Carden Esqr. Commander Is respectfully inscribed to Capt. Stephen Decatur his Officers and Gallant Crew by their devoted humble Servant

Plate 54 *The United States Capturing the Macedonian* (Seymour)

Plate 55 *The United States and Macedonian*

James Webster. Fought Oct[r.] *25*[th.] *1812 The Macedonian had 36 killed and 68 wounded The United States had 5 killed and 7 wounded.*

Painted by T. Birch, A.C.S.A. Engraved by S. Seymour Phil[a.] *Published 20*[th.] *May 1815 by James Webster. Subscription Price $5.00.*

Vignette at bottom of left profile of Decatur.
Line engraving 25¾″ by 18″. Colored by hand. First state.
Stauffer 2879. Grolier 64. Olds 162.

Plate 55

No. 84

Les Etats Unis Et le Macedonian + The United States and The Macedonian

Chez Lordereau r. S[t.] *Jacques N*[o.] *59 à Paris. Déposé Lith de Betremieux Fecit*

Lithograph. 25⅛″ by 18 1/16″. Colored by hand. Undated. Second state after misspelling of Etats was corrected. Rare in either state.
Grolier 72. Olds 170.

Plate 56

No. 85

Capture of H.B.M. Frigate Macedonian 38 Guns Capt. Carden. By the Frigate United States 44 Guns Commodore Decatur. After a close action of Seventeen Minutes.

At left side:

On board the United States 5 killed. 7 wounded.

At right side:

On board the Macedonian 36 Killed. 68 Wounded.

J.J. Barralet del. S. Seymour sc.

Philad. Publish'd by W. H. Morgan 114 Chestnut Street.

Aquatint. 16⅞″ by 11¼″. Colored by hand.
Fielding 1430. Grolier 66. Olds 164.

Plate 57

No. 86

Prise de la frégate anglaise Macédonian, par la frégate américaine united States.

The English frigate Macedonian Captur'd By the american united States, N[o.] *3.*

Plate 56 *Capture of the Macedonian*

Plate 57 *United States and Macedonian*

Plate 58 *The United States and Macedonian Passing Hurl Gate*

Dessiné par Montardier du Havre. Gravé par Baugean.

A Paris, chez Jean Rue St. Jean de Beauvais No. 10.

Line engraving. 17⅛" by 11½". Colored by hand. Undated. First state.

Olds 169. One of a set of four prints by Baugean after Montardier.

Plate 58 No. 89

United States and Macedonian Frigates passing Hurl Gate for New York.

Being the first British frigate brought into the U. States during the Late War, firing a salute as they pass'd.

Published by P. H. Hansell Carver and Gilder No. 177 Race St. Philadela. 1817.

Line engraving. 18¾" by 11⅞". Black and white. Artist and engraver not named. Hurl Gate is the section of East River now called Hell Gate.

Extremely rare. Not in Olds or Stauffer. Grolier 67, except before coloring.

This engraving was in the Havemeyer collection.

Plate 59 No. 90

The U.S. Frigate United States Stephen Decatur Esqr. Commander Capturing His B. M's Frigate Macedonian October 25th. 1812

Oval line engraving 3 3/16" diameter. Black and white. Engraver unknown. Appears to be after painting by Birch. Unusual.

Plate 60 No. 91

Stephen Decatur Esqr. of the United States Navy

Oval stipple engraving. 3" diameter. Black and white. Artist and engraver not known. Companion piece to No. 90 above.

CONSTITUTION—JAVA

When the *Constitution* arrived in Boston after her triumph over the *Guerriere,* her captain's joy at the adulation of his countrymen was soon mitigated by his brother's death and then the news of his uncle's surrender at Detroit. General William Hull, a veteran of the Revolution, had lost his ardor, and his conduct of the campaign in Michigan was timid and di-

Plate 59 *The United States Capturing His B.M.'s Frigate Macedonian*

Plate 60 *Portrait of Stephen Decatur*

sastrous. Isaac Hull's brother's death meant that additional responsibility fell on him, so accordingly he requested relief from sea duty. Command of the *Constitution* went to Captain William Bainbridge, who by this time was determined to make up for the surrender of the *Philadelphia* in the war with Tripoli and the *Retaliation* in the war with France.

Flushed with a feeling of success, the Navy Department formed a squadron under Bainbridge, consisting of the *Constitution, Hornet,* and *Essex.* The scheme was to cruise into the Indian Ocean via the Cape of Good Hope. The *Essex,* under Captain David Porter, an officer of the Decatur type, managed to get off on her own, because of inability to rendezvous with the *Constitution.* That left the *Hornet,* but Bainbridge assigned her to blockade HMS *Bonne Citoyenne* at St. Salvador, Bahia, Brazil.

The *Constitution* then made for the trade route to India, and in very short order she sighted a ship of her own size, which turned out to be the *Java,* Captain Lambert. The two ships then closed for action on 29 December, 1812.

The fight which ensued was as hot and heavy as any single ship action of the war. The *Java* lost her foremast, main topmast, and gaff and then her spanker and mizzen. In the exchange of shot the *Constitution* suffered thirty casualties, but the *Java* lost well over one hundred. Bainbridge outmaneuvered her and raked her fore and aft, broadside after broadside. Captain Lambert was mortally wounded, and his First Lieutenant Chad finally saw no point in prolonging the slaughter and surrendered.

Bainbridge received Captain Lambert's sword on the quarter deck of the *Constitution.* He then ordered the *Java* to be burned and took the prisoners into St. Salvador for exchange. While in this neutral port he returned the sword to the gallant British captain while the latter lay in his cot aboard the *Constitution.* Lambert was carried ashore where he succumbed to his wounds. Bainbridge's humane treatment of the prisoners was given high praise and duly noted even by the Admiralty in London.

After the conclusion of this engagement and the inability to rendezvous with the *Essex,* Bainbridge decided to return to Boston. He returned to find that this was the third, not second, major frigate victory, Decatur having returned with his prize. In any event, Commodore Bainbridge justly received the wild plaudits of the townspeople of Boston and indeed the nation as the news spread.

Plate 61 *The Constitution and Java,* Scene 1

Plate 62 *The Constitution and Java,* Scene 2

Plate 61

No. 92

Dedicated by Permission to the Right Honourable the Lords Commissioners of the Admiralty.

Plate 1. Situation of His Majesty's Frigate Java, Captain Lambert, at 5 Min. past 3 P.M. after an hours close & severe Action with the American Frigate Constitution, in which she was so much disabled in her Masts, Sails & Rigging, by the Enemy's very superior Force & Weight of Metal, that in the attempt to Board, with every prospect of success, her Foremast fell, & she was rendered totally unmanageable.

Drawn & Etch'd by N. Pocock, from a Sketch by Lieut. Buchanan.

Engraved by R. & D. Havell. Jany. 1, 1814, Publish'd by Messrs. Boydell & Co. No. 90 Cheapside, and Colnaghi & Co. Cockspur Street, London.

Statement of the number of men and armament of each ship at the sides.
Aquatint. 19 15/16″ by 14″. Colored by hand. Proof.
Grolier 77. Olds 181. First of a set of four prints by R. & D. Havell.

Plate 62

No. 93

Dedicated by Permission to the Right Honourable the Lords Commissioners of the Admiralty.

Plate 2nd. The Java, as she appeared at 35 Min. past 4 P.M. after having sustained several raking Broadsides from the Constitution whilst closely engaging her, untill she became a perfect Wreck, the Main Mast alone standing, the Rigging shot to pieces, and the Main Yard gone in the Slings, The Constitution making Sail & getting out of Gun Shot.

Drawn & Etch'd by N. Pocock, from a Sketch by Lieut. Buchanan.

Engraved by R. & D. Havell. Jany. 1, 1814. Publish'd by Messrs. Boydell & Co. No. 90 Cheapside, and Colnaghi & Co. Cockspur Street, London.

Statement of the number of men and armament of each ship at the sides.
Aquatint. 17 15/16″ by 14 1/16″. Colored by hand. Proof.
Grolier 78. Olds 182. Second of the set of four prints engraved by Havell.

Plate 63

No. 94

Dedicated by Permission to the Right Honourable the Lords Commissioners of the Admiralty.

Plate 3d. The Java totally dismasted endeavouring to Wear by the assistance of a Jury Staysail hoisted to the Stump of the Foremast & Bowsprit; the Con-

Plate 63 *The Constitution and Java,* Scene 3

Plate 64 *The Constitution and Java,* Scene 4

stitution Crossing her Bow in a Raking Position, Compels her to Surrender at 50 Min. past 5.

Drawn & Etch'd by N. Pocock, from a Sketch by Lieut. Buchanan.

Engraved by R. & D. Havell. Jany. 1, 1814, Publish'd by Messrs. Boydell & Co. 90 Cheapside and Colnaghi & Co. Cockspur Street, London.

Aquatint. 18″ by 14″. Colored by hand. Proof.
Grolier 79. Olds 183.
Third of the set of four prints engraved by Havell.

Plate 64

No. 95

Dedicated by Permission to the Right Honourable the Lords Commissioners of the Admiralty.

Plate 4th. The Java in a Sinking state, set fire to, & Blowing up. The Constitution at a distance ahead, Laying to, unbending Sails, repairing her Rigging & c. on the Evening of 29th. Decr. 1812.

Drawn & Etch'd by N. Pocock, from Sketch by Lieut. Buchanan.

Engraved by R. & D. Havell. Jany. 1, 1814. Publish'd by Messrs. Boydell & Co. Cheapside, and Colnaghi & Co. Cockspur Street, London.

Statement of the number of men and armament of each ship at the sides.
Aquatint. 17⅞″ by 14″. Colored by hand. Proof.
Grolier 80. Olds 184.
Fourth of the set of four prints engraved by Havell.

Plate 65

No. 96

To Commodore Bainbridge the officers Seamen & Marines of the United States frigate Constitution this view of their Glorious capturing the British frigate the Java off the coast of Brazils on the 29th. Xber 1812 after a Sanguinary conflict of 1 hour & 55 minutes, is with respect dedicated to them & the sons of freedom by an admirer of American Valour & patriotism.

Eagle in center of title.

Drawn under the direction of a witness of the action by W. G.

Artist not otherwise identified. Engraver and publisher not named.
Aquatint. 18¼″ by 12⅞″. Colored by hand. Undated.
Grolier 81. Olds 185.

Plate 65 *View of the Glorious Capture of the Java*

Plate 66 *Naval Combat — Glorious Capture of the Java*

Plate 66

No. 97

Le Combat Naval.—Gloire Américaine.

Pris glorieuse, du Vaisseau Anglais la Java, par la constitution, frégate Américaine, sur les côtes du Brézil, le 29 7bre. 1812; après un combat sanglant d'une heure 55 minutes.

Garneray del. Coqueret sc.

A Paris chez Bulla, Rue St. Jacques No. 33. Déposé.

Aquatint. 18⅜" by 12 15/16". Colored by hand. Undated.
Olds 186.

No. 98

Le Combat Naval.—Gloire Américaine.

Pris glorieuse, du Vaisseau Anglais la Java, par la constitution, frégate Américaine, sur les côtes du Brézil, le 29 7bre. 1812; après un combat sanglant d'une heure 55 minutes.

Garneray del. Coqueret sc.

A Paris chez M. Guerin vieille rue du Temple No. 75. Déposé.

Aquatint. 18½" by 13⅛". Black and white.

Plate 67

No. 99

Pris de la frégate anglaise Java, par la frégate américaine le Constitution.

The English Java, Captur'd, By the american frigate Constitution.

"No. 1" in upper right hand corner of margin.

Dessiné par Montardier du Havre Gravé par Baugean

A Paris, chez Jean, rue St. Jean de Beauvais, No. 10.

Line engraving. 16⅞" by 10⅞". Colored by hand. Undated. First state.
Grolier 84. Olds 190 is second state with Baugean spelled Baujean. Fourth in a set of four engravings by Baugean after Montardier.

No. 100

Constitution And Java. Fought Dec. 29th. 1812. The Constitution had 9 killed & 25 wounded. The Java had 60 killed & 170 wounded.

Entered according to Act of Congress in the year 1846 by N. Currier, in the Clerk's office of the District Court of the Southern District of N.Y.

Plate 67 *The English Java Captured by the Constitution*

Plate 68 *Portrait of Commodore Bainbridge*

Lith. & Pub. by N. Currier. 2 Spruce St. N.Y.

Lithograph. 13″ by 7⅞″. Colored. Undated.
Olds 193. Grolier 86, this being the Grolier copy.

No. 101

William Bainbridge Esq.

Commodore in the U.S. Navy

Williams pinx. I.R. Smith, sculp.

Stipple engraving. Oval 4″ by 3″. Colored by hand.

Plate 68 No. 102

W. Bainbridge, Esqr. U.S.N.

Stuart Pinxt. Edwin Sculpt.

Published by M. Thomas Philaa.

Vignette below of the engagement between the *Constitution* and the *Java* inscribed "Kearney delt. et sculpt."
Full bust portrait in uniform, without hat. Face turned slightly toward right.
Stipple engraving. Rectangle. 4¾″ by 3 11/16″. Black and white. Undated.
Stauffer 708. Olds 436.

Irving Olds was not correct in listing this print in Fielding's nor as Grolier 232. The latter did not have the publication line. However, his assertion that this was engraved for *The Analectic Magazine* in 1813 is most probably correct, judging from the work Edwin was doing at that time. My source is Fielding's.

HORNET AND PEACOCK

While the *Hornet* was on station off St. Salvador blockading the *Bonne Citoyenne*, a British 74, HMS *Montagu*, hove into sight, obviously bent on relieving the *Bonne Citoyenne* from her siege. As night was falling while the *Montagu* was on station, the *Hornet*, under Master Commandant James Lawrence, slipped out to sea unmolested.

On her cruise northward on 24 February, 1813, she fell in with a brig of comparable size, HMS *Peacock*. In the ensuing battle the *Peacock* was cut to pieces and in fifteen minutes sank. There apparently was no way the British could match the American effectiveness in gunnery, and that held true throughout the war.

James Lawrence, who in his next battle joined the list of fallen American heroes, displayed his true character after the *Peacock* struck by his strenuous efforts to save the lives of the enemy who were otherwise doomed to drown. In fact he lost more men trying to save the *Peacock* than in the battle itself.

After the battle the *Hornet* set sail for home, arriving at Martha's Vineyard on the 19th of March. Thence she proceeded to New York via Long Island Sound. Lawrence was promptly promoted to captain and ordered to Boston to take command of the ill-fated *Chesapeake.*

No. 103

The Hornet Blockading The Bonne Citoyenne.

M. Corne, p. A. Bowen, sc.

Woodcut 6¾″ by 3⅜″.
Illustration from an edition of *The Naval Monument.*

No. 104

Hornet Sinking the Peacock

M. Corne, p. A. Bowen, sc.

Woodcut 6¾″ by 3 3/16″. Hand colored.
Another illustration from *The Naval Monument.*

PROCEEDINGS OF DIPLOMACY

Early in the war, Russia offered to mediate between the United States and Britain. In March of 1813 the offer of the Czar was accepted by the States but rejected by Britain, despite the fact that the British nation had been at war for twenty years and was clearly unsympathetic to further combat with former colonies, especially people of the same blood. Leading the opposition to the war was again Lord Castlereagh. Further American depredations on British shipping, by both warship and privateer, served to strengthen the argument for settlement. Accordingly Britain invited direct negotiations, to which the United States sent Henry Clay and other representatives. Negotiations lasted all of the year 1814, culminating in the Treaty of Ghent, signed on Christmas Eve of that year.

The Treaty simply brought an end to hostilities. Matters of moment, such as impressment, blockade rights, fishing rights, navigation rights, territorial matters, and all the nettling differences over which blood had been spilt were no more than deferred. But at least the war, which should not have started, was finally stopped by negotiation.

One caricature engraving which referred to the Russian offers of mediation was published by Charles in Philadelphia and, while perhaps frivolous, nevertheless represents one of the unusual episodes of our history. It illustrated the efforts toward peace which began early in 1813.

Plate 69 No. 105

Bruin become Mediator or Negotiation for Peace.

A brown bear is depicted between John Bull (with horns growing out of his head) and a fair lady carrying the American flag. John Bull says, "Pray Mr. Bruin try if you can make up this Little Difference between us—The *Wasps* and *Hornets* have stung me so hard I wish I had never disturbed their nests." Mr. Bruin says, "Let me unite your hands Madam—Johnny and I have been very friendly since I sent him my Fleet to take care of." The American queen, with a crown bearing 76 on the front, says, "I thank you Mr. Bruin but I cannot trust the Bull. 'Tho he has promised to draw in his horns he must be safe bound to the Stake before I treat with him."

Wm. Charles, del et Sculp.

Line etching combined with aquatint. 12 11/16" by 8 5/16". Colored by hand. Undated.

Very rare. Not in Olds. Stauffer 327.

CHESAPEAKE — SHANNON
1 JUNE, 1813

The unlucky *Chesapeake* of Commodore James Barron fame, having returned from a long cruise without success, was lying in Boston. Her skipper Captain Evans had lost the sight of one eye and requested transfer ashore. James Lawrence, who had been promoted to captain after his bril-

Plate 69 *Negotiation for Peace*

liant feats with the *Hornet,* was put in command of this unfortunate ship.

HMS *Shannon,* Captain Broke, was on station off Boston spoiling for a duel with the *Chesapeake.* The latter's orders were to clear the coast and rendezvous with the *Hornet,* Captain James Biddle, in Nova Scotia waters and then to disrupt the Greenland fishery. With a shortage of seasoned officers and a sullen crew, Captain Lawrence was under no illusion about his situation. Nevertheless he got under way, knowing the *Shannon* was waiting for him.

The action which followed is famous in American history not for the performance of crew but for the bravery of Captain Lawrence, whose dying words were, "Don't give up the ship." In all other respects the engagement was a lopsided victory for the British over a crew which for the most part stayed below decks. Even with the personnel he had, Lawrence might still have won the battle had it not been for one bad break, hooking her mizzen rigging in the *Shannon*'s chains. This put the *Chesapeake* stern-to, and the *Shannon* raked her decks with carronades. Captain Lawrence, before being wounded, called for boarders but none could be mustered.

James Lawrence was born in Burlington, New Jersey. His father was a prominent lawyer. He was highly respected by his peers and subordinates as both an officer and a gentleman, and his gallantry has been an inspiration for generations of naval officers.

The captured *Chesapeake* was taken as a prize to Halifax and great importance was attached to this victory in Britain. Indeed, Captain Broke was knighted; his country needed a means of saving face.

Plate 70 No. 106

This view of his Majesty's Ship Shannon, hove too, & cooly waiting the close approach of the American Frigate Chesapeake, who is bearing down to the Attack, with all the confidence of Victory with its Companion the Capture of the Enemy; is with all due respect, & admiration of their intrepid conduct, most respectfully inscribed to Captain P.B.V. Broke and his gallant Ships Company, by their Obed^t. Servant Robt. Dodd.

Painted by R. Dodd from the information of Captn. Falkinir.

Published August. 1813, by R. Dodd, N°. 3 Lucas Place, Commercial Road and G. Andrews, N°. 7, Charing Cross.

Plate 70 *The Shannon Waiting the Approach of the Chesapeake*

Plate 71 *The Boarding of the Chesapeake*

Plate 72 *Commencement of the Action between Shannon and Chesapeake*

Plate 73 *The Boarding and Capture of the Chesapeake*

First of a pair of aquatints by Robert Dodd. 18¼″ by 13″. Colored by hand. First state.

Grolier 95. Olds 201.

Plate 71

No. 107

To Captain P.B.V. Broke commanding his Majesty's Ship Shannon, his Officers, Seamen & Marines, this representation of their gallantly boarding the American Frigate Chesapeak, being 110 Men superior in force and hauling down the Enemy's Colours in fifteen Minutes from the commencement of the Action Is most respectfully Inscribed by their Obt. Servant Robt. Dodd.

Painted by Robt. Dodd, from the information of Captn. Falkinir.

Published August, 1813, by R. Dodd, No. 3, Lucas Place, Commercial Road and G. Andrews, No. 7, Charing Cross.

Second of a pair of aquatints by Robert Dodd. 18¼″ by 13″. Colored by hand. First state.

Grolier 96. Olds 202.

Plate 72

No. 108

To that distinguished Nobleman from whose Precepts & Example the British Navy has derived its present unrivalled state of Discipline and Glorious Preeminence John Earl of St. Vincent, K.B. late first Lord Commissioner of the Admiralty, Admiral of the Red, Lieut. General of Marines, &c—This view of the Commencement of the Action between His Majesty's Ship Shannon and the United States Frigate Chesapeake, off Boston Light House, on the 1st. of June, 1813, is respectfully Dedicated by his Lordship's obedient Servt. G. Webster.

At left:

Shannon, 48 Guns—330 Men, Killed 23 Wounded 56

At right:

Chesapeake, 49 Guns—440 Men, Killed 70 Wounded 100

Painted by John Theophilus Lee Esqr. Joseph Jeakes sculpt.

London, Published by G. Webster & Co. 21 White Lion Street, Pentonville, & Sold by R. Lambe, Printseller, 96, Gracechurch Street.

First of a pair of aquatints by Joseph Jeakes after John Theophilus Lee. This is the second state, with the word "Preeminence" spelled correctly. 21⅞″ by 15¾″. Colored by hand. Not dated.

Grolier 97. Olds 204.

Plate 73

No. 109

To Captain Broke, the Officers, Seamen and Marines of His Majesty's Ship, Shannon, This View of their Boarding & Capturing the American United States Frigate The Chesapeake, off Boston, on the 1st. of June, 1813, after a sanguinary Conflict of only fifteen minutes—is with respect Dedicated to them, and the Admirers of British Valor, by their obedient Servant, G. Webster.

Painted by G. Webster under the direction of Captn. Falkner, late Lieut. of the Shannon during the Action. Jeakes sculpt.

Published by G. Webster, 21, White Lion Street, Penton-Ville.

Statement of armament, crew, and losses given on each side.

Second of a pair of aquatints by Joseph Jeakes after John Theophilus Lee. 21¾" by 15½". Colored by hand. Not dated. First state.

Grolier 98. Olds 205.

Plate 74

No. 110

To the Right Honorable Lord Viscount Melville first Lord of the Admiralty This print of His Majesty's Frigate the Shannon, Captn. Broke, Commander, carrying the American Frigate, Chesapeake, (Commanded by Capt. Lawrence) by boarding in sight of Boston Harbour is respectfully inscribed by His Lordship's Most obedient and devoted Humble Servants J. Hassell, & Co.

At right:

Chesapeake 49 Guns and 440 Men—Shannon 38 Guns and 330 Men

Painted by Thos. Whitcombe Aquaa. Jeakes

Aquatint. 21" by 15⅛". Colored by hand.

Contrary to Olds, the writer believes this copy with no publisher's line to be first state. Mr. Olds had both copies but he lists the one with the publisher's line as first state.

Plate 75

No. 111

No. 1 To Captain Sir Philip Bowes Vere Broke, Bart. and K.C.B. This representation of H.M.S. Shannon, commencing the Battle with the American Frigate Chesapeake, on the 1st. of June 1813, is Dedicated by his obliged and most grateful Servant, R.H. King.

Painted by J.C. Schetky Esqre. & on Stone by L. Haghe. Designed by Captn. R.H. King, R.N.

Plate 74 *Boarding of the Chesapeake*

Plate 75 *The Chesapeake and Shannon,* Scene 1

Plate 76 *The Chesapeake and Shannon,* Scene 2

London, Pubd. by Smith, Elder & Co. 65, Cornhill. Printd. by W. Day, 17, Gate St.

The first of a set of four English lithographs. 16⅞″ by 12″. Colored by hand. Undated.
Grolier 101. Olds 208.

Plate 76 No. 112

No. 2 To Captain Sir Philip Bowes Vere Broke, Bart. and K.C.B. This representation of the American Frigate Chesapeake, Crippled and thrown into utter disorder by the two first broadsides fired from H.M.S. Shannon, is Dedicated by his obliged and most grateful Servant, R.H. King.

Painted by J.C. Schetky Esqre. & on Stone by L. Haghe. Designed by Capt. R.H. King R.N.

London Pubd. by Smith, Elder & Co. 65 Cornhill.

Printd. by W. Day, 17, Gate St.

The second of a set of four lithographs. 16⅝″ by 12⅛″. Colored by hand. Undated.
Grolier 102. Olds 209.

Plate 77 No. 113

No. 3 To Captain Sir Philip Bowes Vere Broke, Bart. and K.C.B. This representation of H.M.S. Shannon, carrying by Boarding the American Frigate Chesapeake, after a Cannonade of Five Minutes, on the 1st. June, 1813 is Dedicated by his obliged and most grateful Servant, R.H. King.

Painted by J.C. Schetky Esqre. & on Stone by L. Haghe.

Designed by Capt. R.H. King, R.N.

London Pubd. by Smith, Elder & Co. 65 Cornhill. Printd. by W. Day 17, Gate St.

The third of a set of four lithographs. 16½″ by 12⅛″. Colored by hand. Undated.
Grolier 103. Olds 210.

Plate 78 No. 114

No. 4 To Captain Sir Philip Bowes Vere Broke, Bart. and K.C.B. This representation of H.M.S. Shannon leading her Prize the American Frigate Ches-

Plate 77 *The Chesapeake and Shannon*, Scene 3

Plate 78 *The Chesapeake and Shannon*, Scene 4

apeake, into Halifax Harbour, on the 6th. June, 1813, is Dedicated by his obliged and most grateful Servant, R.H. King.

Painted by J.C. Schetky Esqre. & On Stone by L. Haghe.

Designed by Capt. R.H. King, R.N.

London Pubd. by Smith, Elder & Co. 65 Cornhill. Printed by W. Day, 17 Gate St.

The fourth of a set of four lithographs. 16¾″ by 12⅛″. Colored by hand. Undated.
Grolier 104. Olds 211.

No. 115

Boarding and Taking the American Ship Chesapeake, by the Officers & Crew of H. M. Ship Shannon, Commanded by Capt. Broke, June 1813.

Heath delt. M. Dubourg sculpt.

Published & Sold July 1, 1816, by Edwd. Orme, Publisher to His Majesty, & the Prince Regent, Bond Street, corner of Brook Street, London.

Aquatint. 10¾″ by 7 11/16″. Colored by hand.
Grolier 108. Olds 220.

Plate 79

No. 116

The Capture of The American Frigate the Chesapeake. This Action was fought June 1 1813 near Boston in America when after a desperate Engagement of only Fifteen minutes, the Americans were compell'd to Surrender to His Majestys Frigate the Shannon, Commanded by Cap. P.B.V. Broke The Chesapeake was Commanded by Cap. Laurence & had 70 killed & 100 wounded the Shannon had 23 killed & 56 wounded.

Pubd. July 21, 1813 by Geo. Thompson 43 Long Lane West Smithfield.

Line engraving. 8⅛″ by 5½″. Colored by hand. Artist and engraver not named.
Extremely rare. Not in Olds or Grolier.

Plate 80

No. 117

James Lawrence Esqr.
Late of the United States Navy.

Stuart pinxt. Edwin sct.

Published by Moses Thomas, Philada.

Entered according to Act of Congress Dec. 1813.

Drawn and engraved by F. Kearney.

Stipple engraving. 4¾" by 3¾". Black and white. Vignette below engraving.

Plate 81

No. 118

The Death of Capt. James Lawrence on board the Chesapeake June 1st. 1813.

Engraved by R. Rawdon.

On a ribbon across the mast is inscribed "Don't Give Up the Ship."
Line engraving. 13¾" by 9 11/16". Black and white.
Rare. Not in Olds. Stauffer 2641. Ex F.S. Hicks Collection.

No. 119

Death of Captain Lawrence. "Don't Give Up The Ship."

Painted by Alonzo Chappel.

Entered according to Act of Congress A.D. 1867 by Johnson Fry & Co. in the clerk's office of the district court of the southern district of New York.

Line engraving. 6¾" by 5½". Colored by hand.
Olds 231.

No. 120

An Improved Map of the United States by Shelton & Kensett

Engraved by A. Doolittle New Haven

Published by Shelton & Kensett, Cheshire Connect. Novr. 8th. 1813

At top:

Copy right secured, & entered according to act of Congress Novr. 8th. 1813.

Nine small vignettes of naval engagements of the War of 1812 are at the right in the Atlantic Ocean, entitled "U.S. Frigate Constitution 44G. Hull taking the British Frigate Guerriere Capt. Dacres August 12th. 1812"; "U.S. Frigate Chesapeake 36G. Lawrence taken by the B. Frigate Shannon 44 Capt. Broke June 1st. 1813—In this action the Brave & Gallant Lawrence lost his life!"; "U.S. Frigate Essex 30G. Porter taking the British Sloop of War Allert August 13th. 1812"; "U.S. Sloop of War Wasp Capt. Jones taking the B.S. of War Frolick Capt. Winyates Oct. 18th. 1812"; "U.S. Frigate Constitution Com. Bainbridge taking the British Frigate Java C. Lambert Decr. 29th. 1812"; "U.S. Sloop of War Hornet Capt. Lawrence taking the British Sloop of War Peacock Capt.

Plate 79 *The Chesapeake and Shannon*

Plate 80 *Portrait of James Lawrence*

Plate 81 *The Death of Captain Lawrence*

Peak Feb. 27th. 1813"; "U.S. Frigate United States Com. Decatur taking the British Frigate Macedonian, Capt. Carden Oct. 25th. 1812"; "Memorable Action fought by Com. Perry on the 10th. of Sept. 1813 in which the whole of the British force, on Lake Erie, was captured"; and "U.S. Sloop of War Argus Capt. Allen taken by the B. Man of War Brig Pelican Capt. Maples August 12th. 1813."

At the sides are the distances by post roads between various communities. At the bottom are notes covering the population and principal products of the different states.

Line engraving. 19¼" by 17 9/16". Black and white. Third state.

Fielding 355. Grolier 216. Olds 395. The Olds impression of this map contains seven small vignettes and was published in July 1813 rather than November. This edition added Perry's victory, September 1813, and the *Argus-Pelican* duel of 12 August, 1813.

ARGUS AND PELICAN
13 AUGUST 1813

This engagement between brigs in the Irish Sea would call for little note except that the *Argus* Captain, William Henry Allen, formerly first lieutenant under Decatur and a lieutenant in the *Chesapeake* under Barron, was a most unusual officer and gentleman. Allen's respect for humanity, his treatment of his own men and also his captives, was remarkable in an otherwise tough and exacting service. He enjoyed the highest repute among friend and foe alike.

The *Argus* left the coast of Brittany and ranged up and down the Channel and into the Irish Sea. She had captured and destroyed twenty merchantmen. The last one had been loaded with wine, much of which was believed to have been transferred to the warship. This act may have had an unfortunate effect on her performance against the enemy.

When overhauled by HMS *Pelican,* carrying twenty-five percent heavier armament, the *Argus* was manned by a tired crew, possibly under the influence of wine from her most recent capture. Early in the ensuing fight Allen was hit and later died of his wounds ashore. Being outgunned and outmaneuvered by the *Pelican,* the *Argus* was forced to strike. Allen, whose feats along the English coast were comparable to Wickes, Conyngham, and Jones, was buried with full honours, having officers of both the United States Navy and the Royal Navy as pallbearers.

Plate 82 *Capture of the Argus*

Plate 82

No. 121

Capture of the Argus, Augt. 14th. 1813.

Publish'd Feby. 1—1817, at 48 Strand, for J. Jenkins's Naval Achievements.

Painted by T. Whitcombe. Engraved by T. Sutherland.

Aquatint. 10⅜″ by 6¾″. Colored by hand. Undated.
Grolier 116. Olds 232.

ENTERPRISE AND BOXER

The U.S. brig *Enterprise,* Lieutenant William Burrows commanding, left Portsmouth, N.H., on 1 September, 1813, in search of privateers. She soon discovered the British brig *Boxer.* After a fight of forty minutes the *Boxer* surrendered. Both captains had received mortal wounds in the combat. Subsequently the two captains were buried in Portland, Maine, side by side.

No. 122

The Enterprise and Boxer

M. Corne p. A Bowen sc

Woodcut. 6¾″ by 3¼″. Colored by hand. Undated.

No. 123

Capture of the Argus, August 14th. 1813.

Painted by Whitcombe. Engraved by T. Sutherland

At top:
From a painting in the possession of Captn. Maples

Pubd. by Pyall & Stroud, 19, Hanway Street, Oxford Strt.

Aquatint. 8 3/16″ by 5¼″. Colored by hand.
Rare. Not in Olds or Grolier. Ex Havemeyer collection.

ACTION ON THE LAKES

In an effort to support the American military campaign against the British in the north, Captain Isaac Chauncey was sent to Lake Ontario in 1813 to supervise the building of a fleet and to command it. Then in another related move Oliver Hazard Perry, a master commandant, was given command of naval forces on Lake Erie. Similarly, the British hurried to build fleets on both lakes; the one on Lake Ontario was commanded by Vice-Admiral Sir James Yeo, the one on Lake Erie by Lieutenant Robert Barclay. In each case the Lake Erie squadrons were commanded by officers subordinate to the commanders on Lake Ontario.

No major action took place on Lake Ontario, although Chauncey's movements greatly supported the military actions mounted in that area. On Lake Erie, however, the two fleets met in a decisive battle.

At first, the American flagship *Lawrence,* named after Captain Lawrence of the *Chesapeake* and flying a flag with the motto "Don't Give Up The Ship"—Lawrence's dying words—took the full brunt of the enemy's firepower. With the *Lawrence* in crippled condition, Perry transferred his flag by gig to the *Niagara,* Master Commandant Elliot. The latter, an enigmatic officer who figured in many controversies, had held the *Niagara* out of the action when she should have come to the early assistance of the *Lawrence.*

When Perry transferred to the *Niagara,* the complexion of the battle soon changed. She quickly overcame the enemy and the latter surrendered. Perry sent his famous message: "We have met the enemy and they are ours." General William Henry Harrison's forces, when they heard this news, attacked and captured Amhurstburg on the north side of the lake. This naval action combined with the military operation under General Harrison put the whole British Canadian campaign in jeopardy.

More important nationally, the news of victory on Lake Erie gave a stimulus to the administration in Washington, upon whom criticism was being heaped for its prosecution of the war. This national need for good news was undoubtedly the reason that Perry's victory was given such prominence—perhaps the greatest acclaim of all the naval actions of this war.

Plate 83 *The Battle of Lake Erie,* Scene 1

Plate 84 *The Battle of Lake Erie,* Scene 2

Plate 83 | No. 124

This representation of the Battle on Lake Erie, is respectfully inscribed, to Commodore Perry, his Officers and gallant Crews; By their humble Servant, James Webster.

Drawn by Sully and Kearny Engrd. by Murray Draper Fairman and Co. Fought Sept. 10, 1813.

Philada. Published 26 July 1815 by Murray Draper Fairman & Co. and J. Webster. Entered according to Act of Congress the 26 July 1815 by Murray Draper Fairman & Co. and J. Webster of the State of Pennsylvania.

Line engraving. 26″ by 17 13/16″. Colored by hand. First state.
Grolier 121. Olds 241.

Plate 84 | No. 125

This representation of the Battle on Lake Erie is respectfully inscribed to Commodore Perry his Officers and gallant Crews By their humble Servant, James Webster.

Drawn by Sully and Kearny Etched by C. Tiebout & Engraved by G. Murray. Fought Sept. 10. 1813.

Philada. Published 26 July 1815 by Murray Draper Fairman & Co. and J. Webster.

Entered according to Act of Congress the 26 july 1815 by Murray Draper Fairman & Co. and J. Webster of the State of Pennsylvania. Second View printed by Rogers & Esler.

Line engraving. 26⅛″ by 18¼″. Colored by hand. Second of a pair. First state.
Grolier 122. Olds 242.

Plate 85 | No. 126

Perry's Victory on Lake Erie.

Published by Joseph Delaplaine.

Painted by T. Birch. Engraved by A. Lawson. Printed by B. Rogers.

Line engraving. 25⅝″ by 18 11/16″. Colored by hand. Undated.
First state. Stauffer 1691i. Grolier 119. Olds 245. Scarce.

Plate 85 *Perry's Victory on Lake Erie* (Lawson)

Plate 86 No. 127

Perry's Victory on Lake Erie, September the 10th. 1813 Represents the position of the two Fleets, at the moment when the Niagara is pushing through the enemy's line, pouring her thunder upon them from both broadsides, and forcing them to surrender in succession to the American Flag. Commodore Perry having a short time before left the Lawrence in a small boat, amidst a tremendous fire from the British Squadron, and hoisted his Flag on board the Niagara. The Lawrence is seen at a distance disabled.

Drawn by J.J. Barralet. Engraved by B. Tanner. Printed by Canmeyer & Acock.

Published 1st. January 1815, by B. Tanner, Engraver, No. 74 South Eighth Street, Philadelphia.

Entered according to Act of Congress the 14th. day of October 1814 by Benjamin Tanner of the State of Pennsylvania.

Line engraving. 24¾″ by 17¼″. Colored by hand. Second state.
Stauffer 3138. Grolier 120. Olds 238.

Plate 87 No. 128

American Naval Victories. Glorious & Brilliant Victory Obtained By Commodore O. H. Perry Over the British Fleet On Lake Erie Commanded By Capt. Barclay. September 10th. 1813.

Oval view at top. Four rectangular views on each side of *Constitution-Guerriere* (two), *United States-Macedonian, Constitution-Java, Wasp-Frolic, Hornet-Peacock, Enterprize-Boxer.*

American school sheet containing poem in the center.

At bottom on flag: "Don't give up the Ship—Lawrence."

N. York Published by J. Tiebout No. 238 Water St. December 1813.

Printed by Riley & Adams 23 Chatham St.

Copy Right Secured According to Law.

Line engraving. 16¼″ by 13½″. Colored by hand.
Fielding 1851. Grolier 124. Olds 251.

Plate 88 No. 129

Sprigs of Laurel

Drawn and engraved by W. Strickland.

Philadelphia. Pub: by John Kneass 125 Market St. Price three Dols.

Plate 86 *Perry's Victory on Lake Erie* (Tanner)

Plate 87 *American Naval Victories*

At the top is a view of Perry's victory. Below that are eight views of naval engagements inscribed as follows:

Constitution and Guerriere, United States and Macedonian, Hornet Blockading Bonne Citoyenne, Enterprise and Boxer, Wasp and Frolic, Constitution and Java, Sinking of the Peacock, Peacock and L'Epervier.

Aquatint. Vignette 19⅞″ by 14½″. Colored by hand. Undated.
Rare. Grolier 212. Olds 396.

No. 130

Battle of Lake Erie, taken 15 Minutes after the commencement of the action.

Statement of names and positions of the ships in each fleet together with their armament.

J. Evans pinxt. On Stone by T.S. Wagner,

P.S. Duval, Lith. Phila. U.S. Military Magazine Army & Navy Vol. 2.

Entered according to act of Congress in the Year 1840, by Huddy and Duval, in the Clerk's Office of the District Court of the Eastern District of Penna.

First of a pair of lithographs. 11″ by 7½″. Colored by hand.
Grolier 134. Olds 270.

No. 131

Battle of Lake Erie. Perry Victorious closing scene of the action.

J. Evans, pinxt. On Stone by J. Queen.

P.S. Duval, Lith. Phila. U.S. Military Magazine Army & Navy Vol. 2nd.

Entered according to act of Congress in the Year 1840, by Huddy & Duval, in the Clerk's Office of the District Court of the Eastern District of Pa.

Second of a pair of lithographs. 10¼″ by 7 5/16″. Colored by hand.
Olds 271. Grolier 135.

No. 132

Naval Heroes of the United States. No. 1 Battle of Lake Erie.

Portraits of Perry, Lawrence, Decatur, Porter, Blakeley and Bainbridge surrounding a view of the Battle of Lake Erie in center.

Lith. & Pub. by N. Currier, 2 Spruce St. N.Y.

Plate 88 *Sprigs of Laurel*

Plate 89 *Perry's Victory on Lake Erie* (Currier)

Entered according to Act of Congress in the year 1846 by N. Currier, in the Clerk's office of the District Court of the Southern District of N.Y.

Lithograph. 12¼″ by 9¼″. Colored by hand.
Grolier 136. Olds 489.

Plate 89

No. 133

Perry's Victory on Lake Erie

Fought Septr. 10th. 1813.

This plate represents the position of the two Fleets at the moment when the NIAGARA is pushing through the enemy's line, pouring her thunder upon them from both broadsides, and forcing them to surrender in succession to the American Flag Commodore Perry having a short time before left the LAWRENCE in a small boat, amidst a tremendous fire from the British Squadron and hoisted his Flag on board the NIAGARA

Below this inscription is Perry's historic message:

"We have met the enemy and they are ours." Com. O. H. PERRY

At left:

Lawrence, killed & wounded 83.

Lith & Pub: by N. Currier, 2 Spruce St. N.Y.

Lithograph. 12½″ by 7⅞″. Colored by hand. Undated.
Grolier 138. Olds 272.

No. 134

Historical chintz, inscribed:

"War Declared Against Great Britain June 12 1812 First Naval Victory Augt. 19 1812. Since which Period until the Signing of the Preliminaries of Peace at Ghent on the 24 Decr. 1814 We Have Taken 1056 Vessels. Huzza Huzza

There is featured in center an oval panel inscribed *Brilliant Naval Victory on Lake Erie Sepr. 15 1814.*
Size 31″ by 28″. Color faded.

No. 135

Battle of Lake Erie

If a victory is to be gained I'll gain it Oliver H. Perry

Painted by W. H. Powell

Entered according to Act of Congress AD 1866 by Johnson Fry & Co. in the Clerk's office of the district court of the southern district of New York

Line engraving. 8″ by 5¾″. Colored by hand.

No. 136

Battle of Lake Erie . . . . . Commodore Perry

Unsigned. Undated. Woodcut. 6″ by 3½″. Colored by hand.

This small print, probably by Abel Bowen for *The Naval Monument,* shows Perry in his gig approaching the *Niagara.* It is the same scene painted by Birch and engraved in an important print by Lawson—No. 126.

Plate 90

No. 137

A Scene on Lake Ontario. United States Sloop of War Gen. Pike, Commodore Chauncey and the British Sloop of War Wolf, sir James Yeo, Preparing for action Sept. 28th. 1813.

R. Rawdon sc.

Published and Sold by Shelton & Kensett Cheshire Con. Novemr. 1st. 1813.

Line engraving. 13⅞″ by 8¼″. Colored by hand.
Olds 285. Grolier 143.

CRUISE OF THE ESSEX

Early in 1813, Captain David Porter of the *Essex* had orders to rendezvous with the *Constitution* and *Hornet* off the Brazilian coast, but the rendezvous never took place. Porter, like Decatur, was known to prefer single ship actions, and there is reason to suspect that he was happy not to have made contact with his Commodore (Bainbridge), who meanwhile had the good fortune to encounter and defeat HMS *Java* in one of the major frigate actions of the war.

On the way south to the Brazilian coast, the *Essex* captured a small brig with $50,000 in specie, which made a long cruise a more viable prospect. Porter, with a little of the buccaneer's avarice, relished the thought

Plate 90 *A Scene on Lake Ontario*

of plundering the British whaling fleet in the Pacific. To this end, he weathered Cape Horn in February 1813. By March, he was at Valparaiso. Since Britain had no warships in the Pacific, her whalers were at Porter's mercy. During the ensuing five months he captured a dozen whalers heavily laden with supplies, money, and rum.

Captain Porter's next adventure was a three-thousand-mile passage to the Marquesas Islands, where his officers and crew wallowed in the pleasures provided by the Polynesian women they found. His avowed purpose was to refit and revictual the ship, but the events that transpired upon his arrival were like a chapter out of *Arabian Nights*. Porter at once cultivated the goodwill of the tribal chief only to find that he had to come to the aid of the chief, who had problems with enemies of another tribe. Finally, Porter annexed the island and renamed it for President Madison.

After stabilizing matters on the island, Porter set sail for Chile, leaving a skeleton crew to guard the prizes. Meanwhile, the British had reacted to these Pacific raids and sent out a squadron to deal with Porter. Two vessels of the British squadron managed to find the *Essex* at Valparaiso, which was a neutral port. The *Essex* and the *Essex Junior* were bottled up there for six weeks; then Porter decided to run the blockade. In the middle of her attempt to escape, the *Essex* was hit by a severe squall which dismasted her. Porter tried to beach his vessel and escape on land but this attempt also failed, and he was finally forced to surrender. In due course Porter and his crew were repatriated and enjoyed a hero's welcome.

Plate 91 — No. 138

Madisonville in Massachusetts Bay—Essex & her Prizes

Drawn by Capt. Porter

Engraved by W. Strickland

Stipple engraving. 6⅞″ by 3⅞″. Black and white.
Not in Olds, Grolier, or Stauffer. William Strickland was a Philadelphia engraver.

No. 139

Capture of the Essex

M. Corne p. A Bowen sc

Plate 91 *The Essex and Her Prizes*

Plate 92 *The Hinchenbrook and Grand Turk*

Woodcut. 6¾″ by 3¼″. Colored by hand. Illustration from *The Naval Monument.* First state.

Grolier 146.

No. 140

Essex and British Frigate in the Harbour of Valparaiso.

Woodcut. 6 9/16″ by 3 11/16″. Colored by hand. Artist and engraver unnamed.

No. 141

David Porter Esqr. of the United States Navy

Stipple engraving. Oval 2¾″ diameter. Colored by hand. Undated.

No. 142

The Peacock and Epervier

T. Birch del. W. Strickland sc.

Woodcut. 6¾″ by 3½″. Colored by hand. Undated.

This was a brig action off the coast of Florida in which the *Peacock,* Captain Lewis Warrington, completely outgunned the British brig, which struck her colors after forty-five minutes.

No. 143

Lewis Warrington Esqr. Of the United States Navy

Jarvis Pinxt. Gimbrede Sculpt.

Engraved for the Analectic Magazine—Published by M. Thomas

Copy Right Secured According to Act of Congress October 2. 1815.

Printed by Rogers & Esler.

Stipple engraving. 3⅞″ by 3¼″. Colored by hand.

Stauffer 1096. Olds 288b.

Plate 92

No. 144

To Francis Freeling Esqr. Secretary to the General Post Office This Plate representing the situation of H.M. Packet Hinchinbrook at the close of an Engagement with the American Privateer, Grand Turk of Salem, on the 1:

of May 1814.—The action commenced at 5hrs. 20min P.M. and continued until 7hrs 30min within pistol shot, during which the Enemy twice laid the Packet aboard but was beaten off; after the failure of the second attempt the Hinchinbrook obtained a raking position, disabled and obliged the Privateer to sheer off Is very respectfully dedicated by his most obedt. humble Servt. Willm. James Commr.

Drawn by W. I. Pocock. Engraved by Baily 46 Tufton Str. Westminster.

Pub. Feb. 1, 1819. by Messrs. Colnaghi & Co. 23 Cockspur Str. for the Proprietor.

Statement of the force, armament, and losses of each ship below the view at the sides.

Aquatint. 17¾″ by 11⅞″. Black and white.

Grolier 200, Olds 361—except not colored. Ex Havemeyer collection.

ATTACK ON FORT OSWEGO

On 6 May, 1814, a British fleet under Captain Sir James Yeo landed a party of Royal Marines and captured the American fort on the southern shore of Lake Ontario. After taking away the stores they set fire to the barracks and departed.

Plate 93 No. 145

Attack on Fort Oswego, Lake Ontario, N. America. May 6th. 1814, Noon. Dedicated to His Majesty's Royal Marine Forces, and those employ'd on the Expedition. Plate 1.

Drawn by I Hewett, Lt. Royal Marines. Engraved by R. Havell.

Position of ships, fort, and troops referred to below view.

London. Published May 1, 1815.

First of a pair of aquatints. 21⅝″ by 15⅝″. Colored by hand. Rare.

Grolier 151. Olds 291.

Plate 94 No. 146

Storming Fort Oswego, by 2nd. Battalion Royal Marines and a party of Seamen; 15m. past Twelve at Noon. Plate 2.

Plate 93 *Attack on Fort Oswego*, Scene 1

Plate 94 *Attack on Fort Oswego,* Scene 2

Plate 95 *Attack on Fort Oswego*

Dedicated to His Majesty's Royal Marine Forces, and those employ'd on the Expedition.

References below to position of troops and ships.

Drawn by I. Hewett, Lieut. Royal Marines. Engraved by R. Havell.

London. Published May 1, 1815.

Aquatint. 21⅛″ by 15⅜″. Colored by hand. Rare.
Grolier 152. Olds 292. The second of a pair of handsome aquatints. This pair came from the Graves collection.

Plate 95 No. 147

Attack on Fort Oswego, on Lake Ontario, North America. May 6th. 1814.

Drawn by Captn. Steele. Engraved by R. Havell & Son.

Published April 8th 1817, for the Proprietor, by R. Havell, 3 Chapel Street, Tottenham Court Road.

Aquatint. 16 1/16″ by 11¼″. Black and white. Rare.
Grolier 153. Olds 293—except not colored. Ex Havemeyer collection.

BRIG ACTIONS

On 28 June, 1814, the *Wasp,* Master Commandant Johnston Blakely, attacked and defeated the British brig *Reindeer* off the coast of England. In September of the same year she fell in with a British squadron and sank the *Avon.* After this action, the *Wasp* proceeded toward the South Atlantic but totally disappeared. The best conjecture is that she was lost in a storm. Later, another warship, the *Epervier,* under command of Lieutenant Shubrick, also disappeared after departing Gibraltar on 12 July, 1815, bound for home with the treaty signed by the Dey of Algiers. Most probably she was also victim of a storm.

No. 148

The Wasp and Reindeer

M. Corne, p. A Bowen sc.

Woodcut. 6 11/16″ by 3 5/16″. Colored by hand. Undated.

No. 149

The Wasp and Avon

M. Corne, p. *A Bowen sc.*

Reference below to the following ships in the picture: *Castilian, Tartarus, Avon, Wasp, Rapid.*
Woodcut. 6¾″ by 3 5/16″. Colored by hand. Undated.

LAKE CHAMPLAIN

In June, 1814, the British embarked on the same strategy as had been employed in the Revolution—attacking southward from Canada with a combined ground and naval force. The American fleet on Lake Champlain under Commodore Thomas MacDonough repulsed and defeated the enemy near Plattsburgh, New York. At the same time ground forces under General Macomb were likewise successful in repelling the British Army under General Sir George Prevost. This combined victory was the turning point of the war. MacDonough's fleet was inferior in armament to the British, but the Americans took clever advantage of the contour of Plattsburgh Bay, forcing the British to expose their ships to broadside fire from anchored vessels. MacDonough's anchoring system enabled his flagship *Saratoga* to kedge around and bring his port batteries into action after the starboard batteries had been nearly put out of action by enemy fire. One by one His Majesty's ships struck colors.

General Sir George Prevost was so discouraged at the loss of his naval support that he felt obliged to withdraw. MacDonough's victory in this war was thus a close analog of Benedict Arnold's achievement at Valcour Island, also in Lake Champlain, in the Revolutionary War.

Plate 96 No. 150

MacDonough's Victory on Lake Champlain, and Defeat of the British Army at Plattsburg by Genl. Macomb, Septr. 11th. 1814.

Painted by H. Reinagle. Engraved by B. Tanner. Printed by Rogers & Esler.

Published 4th. July 1816 by B. Tanner Engraver N°. 74 South Eighth Street Philadelphia.

Plate 96 *MacDonough's Victory on Lake Champlain*

Entered according to Act of Congress the 22nd. day of May, 1816; by Benjamin Tanner of the State of Pennsylvania.

Line engraving. 24⅝" by 16⅞". Colored by hand. First state.
Stauffer 3134. Grolier 159. Olds 298.

No. 151

Com. MacDonough's Victory on Lake Champlain Sepr. 11th. 1814.

M. Corne p. W. Hoogland sc.

Engraved For The Naval Monument (at top)

Entered according to act of Congress Nov. 25th. 1815 by A. Bowen.

Line engraving. 7⅞" by 3⅞". Colored by hand. First state.
Stauffer 1437. Grolier 162. Olds 304a.

No. 152

Commodore McDonnough

Heroe of Lake Champlain

Designed and aquatinted by (no name mentioned).

Number "82" shows below portrait which is a left profile with full bust in uniform without hat.

Pub. by P. Price Jr. Philada.

Aquatint and line engraving. Vignette. 7⅜" by 7½". Black and white. Undated. Olds 477. Grolier 278. Stauffer 481 or 3051. Stauffer attributes one state of this engraving to Dellaker and the other state to Strickland.

Plate 97 No. 153

Battle of Plattsburg Bay. Mc.Donough's Victory. Sept. 11th. 1814.

On Stone by Jas. Queen. P. S. Duval, Lith, Phila.

U.S. Military Magazine. Army & Navy Vol 2nd

Entered according to Act of Congress in the Year 1840, by Huddy & Duval, in the Clerk's Office of the District Court of the Eastern District of Pennsylva.

Lithograph. 10⅞" by 7⅜". Colored by hand.
Grolier 164. Olds 306.

Plate 97 *Battle of Plattsburg Bay*

No. 154

M'Donough's Victory On Lake Champlain. After an Action of 2 Hours, & 2 Minutes.

Pub. by N. Currier, 2 Spruce St. N.Y.

Entered according to Act of Congress A.D. 1846, by N. Currier, in the Clerk's Office of the Dist. Court of the Southn. Dist. of N. York. 6.

Below is a statement of the armaments and losses of the two fleets.

Lithograph 12½″ by 8″. Colored by hand.

Grolier 167. H.T. Peters' Currier & Ives 1137. Olds 308.

No. 155

Battles of Lake Champlain, and Plattsburgh . . . Commodore M'Donough, and General Macomb

Woodcut. 6⅞″ by 3⅝″. Colored by hand. Artist and engraver not named. Undated. Appears to be work of A. Bowen.

Plate 98

No. 156

Naval Heroes of the United States. No. 2 Battle of Lake Champlain.

Oval-shaped portraits of Thomas MacDonough, Charles Stewart, Isaac Hull, William Henry Allen, Jacob Jones, and Joshua Barney, around view in center of MacDonough's Victory on Lake Champlain.

Lith. Pub. by N. Currier, 2 Spruce St. N.Y.

Entered according to Act of Congress in the year 1846 by N. Currier, in the Clerk's office of the District Court of the Southern District of N.Y.

Lithograph. 12¼″ by 9″. Colored by hand. Companion to No. 132.

Grolier 165. H.T. Peters' Currier & Ives 1937. Olds 490.

Plate 99

No. 157

Caricature by William Charles, entitled:

John Bull making a new Batch of Ships to send to the Lakes

Charles del et Sculp

Philada Pubd and sold Wholesale by Wm. Charles.

Enter'd according to act of Congress.

Plate 98 *Naval Heroes of the United States*

A caricature, depicting George III as John Bull putting a peel with a batch of ships into an oven, inscribed: "Patent Oven for Bakeing Ships," below which is an open box marked: "French Dough Trough." Attendant at dough trough is saying: "Begar Mounseer Bull me no like dis new Alliance—Dere be one Yankey Man da call Mac Do-enough Take your Ships by de whole Fleet—You better try get him for I never get Do-enough made at dis rate!!!"

John Bull says in reply: "Ay! What-What-What? Brother Jonathan taken another whole fleet on the Lakes—Must work away—work away—& send some more or He'll have Canada next—"

Another attendant behind John Bull, bearing a tray of cannons, is saying: "Here are more Guns for the Lake service—If ever they do but get there—I hear the last you sent were waylaid by a sly Yankey Fox and the ship being a Stranger he has taken her in—"

A third attendant at the right, holding another tray of ships ready for the oven, is saying: "I tell you what Master Bull—You had better keep both your Ships and Guns at home—If you send all you've got to the Lakes, it will only make fun for the Yankeys to take them—"

The references in these remarks are to MacDonough's Victory on Lake Champlain on 11 September, 1814, and to Perry's Victory on Lake Erie on 10 September, 1813.

Etching. 12¾" by 9 7/16". Black and white. Undated.

Stauffer 315. Olds 431.

CHESAPEAKE SKIRMISHES

The summer of 1814 was a period of increased enemy activity in the Chesapeake. Napoleon having been defeated, the British sent reinforcements to America. Most eastern ports were under blockade and Chesapeake Bay was the scene of harassing actions by fleet and military units, culminating in the burning of the city of Washington and the later successful attack on Baltimore.

American gunboat forces in the Bay were under Captain Joshua Barney of Revolutionary War fame. His forces in the Patuxent River were a deterrent to the superior forces of Britain. Barney conducted a long series of skirmishes at sea, but when the enemy mounted a land attack on the capital, Washington, Barney's seamen and marines fought them off for as long as possible before being outflanked by superior numbers at the Battle of Bladenburgh. The enemy proceeded to Washington and sacked the capital.

On the 12th of September, enemy forces were landed near Baltimore to attack that city, which was much larger and better defended than the capital. It was during the bombardment of Fort McHenry at the entrance of Baltimore Harbor that Francis Scott Key wrote "The Star-Spangled Banner."

The twenty-four-hour bombardment of Fort McHenry did little harm to the fort and the British were turned back and soon retreated. This repulse ended activity in the Chesapeake, as the enemy turned to New Orleans for their next target.

There is an aquatint by John Bower of Philadelphia depicting the bombardment of Fort McHenry. It is quite rare but not exactly a work of art. The writer passed up his first opportunity to purchase it when it was offered by Harry Newman in 1952, but had the good fortune to add it to his collection in 1973.

PRIVATEER ACTION

On the night of 26 September, 1814, an American privateer *General Armstrong* repelled a gun boat attack at Fayol, Azores. This would have been a desultory privateer action but for the fact it delayed a troop convoy bound for New Orleans, which might have led to a British victory instead of defeat at the hands of General Andrew Jackson's men.

No. 158

The American privateer "General Armstrong" Capt. Sam C. Reid. In the Harbour of Fayol (Azores) Oct$^{r.}$ 26$^{th.}$ 1814. Repulsing the attack of 14 boats containing 400 men from the British Ships 'Plantagenet 74' "Rota" 44 and "Carnation" 18 Guns. The "General Armstrong" was 246 tons burthen Carried 6 Nine pounders and a 'Long' Tom (42 pounder,) amid ships and a crew of 90 men. The British loss was 120 killed and 130 wounded—Americans lost 2 killed and 7 wounded.

Lith. and Pub. by N. Currier 152 Nassau Street, N.Y.

Lithograph. 12⅝″ by 8″. Colored by hand. Undated.
Grolier 174. H.T. Peters' Currier & Ives 1132. Olds 320.

Plate 99 *John Bull Making a New Batch of Ships*

Plate 100 *The Hartford Convention*

HARTFORD CONVENTION

An interesting sidelight to military and naval affairs during the War of 1812 was the internal political struggle based entirely on sectional interests. The Federalist Party was turned out of office in 1800 and replaced by a populist party, the Republicans, later to be the Democratic Party. The latter was dominated by agricultural and Western states. The states involved in foreign commerce—all of New England and New York—were solidly Federalist, while Pennsylvania was aligned with the South and the West.

New England claimed that the federal government was crippling all American commerce just to punish Britain for its wartime measures that affected only a portion of our trade. Consequently, the Northeastern states opposed and harassed the federal government in the conduct of the war. The enemy was clever enough to cultivate this schism, allowing commerce to flow in and out of New England ports. To this situation the federal government responded with an embargo.

In furtherance of New England's sectional interests, the Connecticut legislature called a conference in Hartford, which met on 15 December, 1814. After three weeks, resolutions were adopted, mostly of an obstructionist type and not in the national interest. However, after the Battle of New Orleans and the subsequent news of the Treaty of Ghent, which had been signed on December 24, the Hartford Convention and its sponsors were a dead issue.

Plate 100 No. 159

The Hartford Convention or Leap No Leap.

Wm Charles, Sc.

Enter'd according to act of Congress

Caricature by William Charles picturing three delegates representing Massachusetts, Connecticut, and Rhode Island, the states whose representatives primarily made up the Hartford Convention, on a rocky precipice, hesitating to leap across a channel of water into the arms of George III.

The first says, "Poor little I, what will become of me? this leap is of a frightful size—I sink into despondency—"

The second says, "I cannot Brother Mass; let me pray and fast some time longer—little Rhode will jump the first."

The third says, "What a dangerous leap!!! but we must jump Brother Conn—" The British King, on the right, is saying: "O 'tis my Yankey boys! jump in my fine fellows; plenty molasses and Codfish; plenty of goods to Smuggle; Honours, titles and Nobility into the bargain—" At the foot of the rocks is a kneeling figure, presumably that of Timothy Pickering, saying: "I, Strongly and most fervently pray for the success of this great leap which will change my vulgar name into that of my Lord of Essex—God save the King—"

At left is an oval tablet, with a ribbon tied above, inscribed: "This is the produce of the land they wish to abandon," followed by the names on the tablet of "Perry, McDonough, Hull, Decatur, Bainbridge, Jones, Lawrence, Porter, Rogers, Burrows, Blakely,—Pike, Brown, Harrison, Gains, Scott, McComb, Jackson, &—&—&—"

Etching and aquatint. Rectangle. 13⅝" by 8 11/16". Colored by hand. Undated.

Rare. Stauffer 333. Olds 432.

LAUNCHING OF FULTON THE FIRST

Robert Fulton, who was born in Lancaster County, Pennsylvania, was first trained as an artist. Later under the influence of British friends he became a student of mechanics in England. His first work was directed to the development of a submarine and a torpedo. He worked in France where he was encouraged by Napoleon to continue his experiments. Next, urged by his friend, Lord Stanhope, Fulton went to London in 1804, and the British government employed him to develop the torpedo. In 1806, the inventor returned to the States and concentrated on developing a steam boat. Financed by Robert Livingston, Fulton launched the *Clermont* in 1807—"Fulton's Folly"—as the first Albany night boat. She managed the round trip from New York to Albany in sixty-two hours. In October, 1814, the first steam warship, *Fulton the First*—originally *Demologas*—was launched at New York. She was designed primarily for harbor defense and was destroyed by accidental fire on 4 June, 1829.

Plate 101 No. 160

La Fregate À Vapeur Le Fulton, manoeuvrant dans la Rade de New-Yorck. Au loin le Bateau à vapeur, messager du New-huven. Ce Navire construit et destiné pour la défense des Ports, réunit tous les avantages qui peuvent le rendre redoutable à la Flote qui oseroit insulter la Rade. Sans mats, ni voiles il ne peut être, dégrée; n'ayant besoin ni de vent, ni de marée, il peut

Plate 101 *The Steamship Fulton*

les surmonter l'un et l'autre, manoeuvrant et virant de bord avec beaucoup de velocité, il atteint l'ennemi par le côte qu'il désire, sans qu'il soit possible de l'éviter, sa coque ayant quatre pieds et demi d'espaisseur de plein bois, ne peut être percée par aucun boulet, enfin une artillerie de trente huit pièces du plus gros calibre achèvent de rendre sa défense, la plus formidable, que le génie de l'homme ait pu jamais concevoir.

A Paris, chez Ostervald l'aine Editeur, Rue de la Parcheminerie, No. 2.

Aquatint. 9 11/16" by 7 1/16". Colored by hand. Undated. Artist and engraver not named.
Olds 400.

English translation of the above is: "The steam frigate Fulton, maneuvering in the New York Harbor. Nearby is the steam packet from New Huven (misspelling). This vessel, constructed and intended for port defense, combines all the advantages which make her formidable to a fleet daring to attack the Harbor. Without masts or sails, she cannot be dismasted; having need for neither wind nor tide, she can overcome both; maneuvering and tacking with great speed, she comes up on the enemy on the desired side, without the enemy's being able to evade her. The hull having a thickness of four and a half feet of wood she can't be pierced by ball, and finally a battery of 38 of the greatest calibre guns makes her more formidable than anything man's genius has ever conceived."

BATTLE OF NEW ORLEANS

The Treaty of Ghent, signed on Christmas Eve of 1814, brought the war to an official close. However, news did not travel fast enough to prevent several actions, the greatest of which was the Battle of New Orleans. The Army had achieved very little success in land warfare against the British, but this battle was the exception. It was a crushing and overwhelming defeat which Andrew Jackson inflicted on the attackers. In this effort he was given crucial support from the Navy's gunboats on the Mississippi River. Out of an attacking force of some ten thousand men, the enemy had twenty-six hundred casualties against eight men killed and thirteen wounded on the American side. Included in the enemy's casualties were the two top generals killed and the third in command severely wounded.

Plate 102 No. 161

Battle of New Orleans and Death of Major General Packenham. On the 8th. of January 1815.

West Del. J. Yeager Sc. Printed by Y. Sourman.

Copy Right Secure'd Accordg. to Law Published by Mc.Carty and Davis, Booksellers, Printers, and Stationers, S.E. corner of Ninth & Race Sts. Philada. July 1817

On each side of the title at the bottom are references to various individuals, etc., keyed to letters on the engraved surface.
Line engraving. 19¼" by 13⅛". Colored by hand.
Stauffer 3433. Olds 427.

POSTWAR ACTIONS

Subsequent to the Battle of New Orleans, three naval engagements were fought, in each of which the combatants had no knowledge that the war was over.

The first battle, 14 January, 1815, came about as a result of Stephen Decatur's determination to break the blockade of the *President* at New York. He sneaked out of the harbor at night and grounded on one of the bars near Sandy Hook. The next morning after extricating his splendid vessel, Decatur was discovered by the British blockading squadron, which had been blown off station by strong northwest winds. At first Decatur tried to escape by running eastward along the Long Island shore. His hull damage from the grounding, plus his extra displacement from excess stores for a long voyage, combined to slow the *President.* The lead ship of the British squadron was HMS *Endymion,* which Decatur proceeded to attack. At first the latter was given a fearful pounding by the broadsides of the *President,* but three other enemy frigates made their appearance in light airs. In these conditions, Decatur knew there was no chance for escape and chose to surrender rather than sacrifice his crew. After the capture the *President* was escorted to Bermuda, where Decatur was paroled.

Plate 103 No. 162

To the Captain, Officers, and Brave Crew of His Majesty's Frigate—Endymion—as an Humble Record of British Skill, and Valour.—This Represen-

Plate 102 *Battle of New Orleans*

tation of the Gallant Action on the 15th. day of January with the United States Ship—President—commanded by Commodore Decatur is Respectfully Inscribed by their most Obedient Servant, Thomas Rickards.

Drawn by an Officer of H.M.R.N.   Hill Aquat

London Published May 1—1815 by Thomas Rickards, 344, Strand.

Statement of the comparative force of the two ships at the left.
Aquatint. 20⅞" by 14⅞". Colored by hand. First state.
Grolier 176. Olds 323.

Plate 104

No. 163

To Captain H. Hope, the Officers, Seamen, and Marines, of His Majesty's Frigate, Endymion, This Print representing the Action with the American United States Frigate, President, on Sunday Evening Jany. 15th. 1815; off Sandy Hook—is respectfully Dedicated by their obedient humble Servants, J. Burr & G. Ballisat.

At left side:

Endymion. 49 Guns, 345 Men.

At right side:

President 58 Guns. 525 Men. Difference 9 Guns & 180 Men.

Painted by T. Buttersworth. Engraved by Jos. Jeakes.

Published as the Act directs, June 1st. 1815, by J. Burr & G. Ballisat. Gracechurch Street, London.

First of a pair of aquatints. 21⅝" by 15¾". Colored by hand. First state.
Grolier 177. Olds 325.

Plate 105

No. 164

To Captain H. Hope, the Officers, Seamen, and Marines of His Majesty's Frigate Endymion, This Print representing the Morning after the Action with the American United States Frigate, President, Jany. 16th. 1815—which lasted two Hours and a half—is respectfully Dedicated by their obedient humble Servants, J. Burr & G. Ballisat.

At left side:

Endymion 12 killed. 14 wounded.

Plate 103 *The President and Endymion*

Plate 104 *Action of the Endymion and President,* Scene 1

Plate 105 *Action of the Endymion and President,* Scene 2

At right side:

President 32 killed. 60 Wounded. amongst the former 1st. 3d. & 4th. Lieuts. & 6 Midshipmen.

Names of the five participating ships below the view.

Painted by T. Buttersworth, the particulars & the position of the Ships, by Lieut. Ormond, of the Endymion. Engraved by J. Jeakes.

Published as the Act directs June 1st. 1815, by J. Burr & G. Ballisat, Gracechurch Street, London.

Second of a pair of aquatints. 21¼″ by 15⅝″. Colored by hand. First state.
Grolier 178. Olds 326.

Plate 106 — No. 165

The Capture of the U.S. Frigate, President, by a British Squadron, under the command of Commodore Hayes, off the Coast of America, January 1815. To Captain Henry Robinson, this print is respectfully dedicated, by his sincere Friend, Captain Wm. Skiddy.

Names of the five participating ships below the view.

Drawn & Lithd. by Saml. Walters, Gt. George St. Liverpool from a sketck by Capt. Wm. Skiddy Day & Haghe Lithrs. to the Queen.

Lithograph. 22⅝″ by 14¼″. Colored by hand. Undated.
Very rare. Grolier 179. Olds 329. This was apparently one of a pair with the *Hornet* and *Penguin.* The date of publication would have to be after 1837 when Victoria ascended the throne. Note the word "sketch" is misspelled.

A month later off the island of Madeira in the Atlantic, the *Constitution*—the famous "Old Ironsides"—under the command of Captain Charles Stewart, engaged in her last battle. She remained undefeated, as she overwhelmed HM Frigate *Cyane* and the sloop *Levant.* The *Cyane* was brought into the U.S. Navy and eventually converted to steam. In the Civil War she was active in the bombardment of Fort Sumter while under the flag command of Admiral Samuel Francis du Pont.

On 28 March, 1815, while cruising in the South Atlantic near Tristan da Cunha, the *Hornet,* Captain James Biddle, attacked and captured HMS *Penguin,* a vessel of comparable armament and complement. A month later, Biddle, who had proceeded into the Indian Ocean still unaware of the peace treaty, encountered HMS *Cornwallis,* a British 74-gun ship-of-the-line, which immediately gave chase. The *Hornet*'s crew heaved overboard her chains, guns, and shot to lighten ship, and after two nights and a day the American sloop managed to escape. Here was an incident that took place fully four months after peace was signed on the previous Christmas Eve. Biddle put in at St. Salvador, Brazil, on 9 June, 1815, and it was not till then that he learned of the treaty. Such was the speed of communication 158 years ago.

Plate 107

No. 166

Capture of H. M. Ships Cyane & Levant, By The U.S. Frigate Constitution. To Chas. Stewart Esqr. His Officers & Crew. This Plate is respectfully dedicated by Huddy & Duval.

Position of the three ships, with their armaments, indicated under the view.

From the Original Painting by Birch. On Stone by Jas. Queen

P.S. Duval Lith. Phila. U.S. Military Magazine, Army & Navy, No. 6, Vol 2nd.

Lithograph. 10⅛" by 7 3/16". Colored by hand. Undated. First state, without the word "most" in the dedication line. Illustration from Vol. 2 No. 6 of *U.S. Military Magazine,* published by Huddy & Duval, Philadelphia, December 1840. Grolier 182. Olds 333.

No. 167

View of the action between the U.S. Frigate Constitution & the British Ships Levant & Cyane.

Names of the three ships below the view.

Aquatinted by Strickland for the Analectic Magazine and Naval Chronicle

Published by M. Thomas Philadelphia.

Aquatint. 7⅜" by 3⅞". Colored by hand. Undated. First state.
Illustration from *The Analectic Magazine and Naval Chronicle,* February 1816.
Stauffer 3045. Grolier 185. Olds 336.

No. 168

To Commodore Charles Stewart, "Old Ironsides" This Song Is Cheerfully Inscribed by His Friend. The Author.

Plate 106 *Capture of the President*

Plate 107 *Capture of H. M. Ships Cyane and Levant*

View above of the naval action between the *Constitution, Cyane,* and *Levant,* with names below of the three ships and their respective commanders.

T. P. Otter, Del. T. Sinclair's Lith. Phil$^{a.}$

Philadelphia Lee & Walker 188 Chestnut St.

The song "Old Ironsides" was copyrighted by Lee & Walker in 1856.
Lithograph. 8⅛" by 7⅞". Colored by hand.
Grolier 186. Olds 338.

No. 169

The Hornet And Penguin.

M. Corne, p. A. Bowen, sc.

Published by Abel Bowen, Boston, 1816, first edition.
Woodcut. 6¾" by 3 5/16". Colored by hand. Undated. First state.
Illustration from *The Naval Monument.*
Grolier 188. Olds 339a.

No. 170

James Biddle Esq$^{r.}$ Of the United States Navy

Wood, del. Gimbrede, Sculp$^{t.}$

Engraved for the Analectic Magazine Published by M. Thomas.

Illustration from *The Analectic Magazine,* November 1815.
Full bust portrait in uniform, without hat. Face front. Stipple engraving.
Rectangle. 3¾" by 3⅛". Colored by hand. Undated.
Stauffer 1037. Grolier 238. Olds 339b.

Plate 108 No. 171

To Commodore James Biddle, Esq$^{re.}$ This Print of H M Sloop of War Penguin, Capt$^{n.}$ Dickinson; Captured Off the Island of Tristan D'Acuna, U.S. Sloop of War, Hornet, J. Biddle, Esq$^{re.}$ Commander on the 23$^{rd.}$ March 1815, after an Action of 22 Minutes, Is most respectfully dedicated by his obedient Servant W$^{m.}$ Skiddy.

Forces of the ships are stated at the sides.

Drawn & Lith. by S. Walters, Liverpool, from a sketck by Capt$^{n.}$ Wm. Skiddy.

Day and Haghe Lith$^{rs.}$ to the Queen.

Lithograph. 16⅜″ by 10⅞″. Undated. Colored by hand.

This is believed to be the second of a pair with No. 158 "Capture of the U.S. Frigate President." Note the spelling of "sketch." The print must have been published after 1837, the date of Queen Victoria's succession.

Very rare. Not in Olds. Similar to Grolier 187.

No. 172

The Hornet's Escape From A British 74.

Woodcut. 6 13/16″ by 3 5/6″. Colored by hand. Undated. Artist and engraver not named. Third state. Illustration from a late edition of *The Naval Monument,* being a reissue of the original woodcut contained in the first edition, inscribed: *M. Corne, p. A. Bowen, sc.*

Grolier 190. Olds 341c.

WAR WITH ALGIERS
1815

On 2 March, 1815, the United States declared war on the Algerian corsairs. Two squadrons, one under Commodore Decatur and one under Commodore Bainbridge, were sent to show the Dey of Algiers that the Americans meant business. As a consequence of this show of force, the Dey signed a treaty of peace on the exact terms dictated by President Madison.

No. 173

Plate 109 *United States Squadron under Com. Bainbridge returning triumphant from the Mediterranean in 1815.*

J.B. Fanning Des. G.G. Smith Sc.

Engraved For The Naval Monument

At bottom are the names in three columns of the thirteen ships comprising the squadron, which returned to the United States in 1815 at the conclusion of the War with Algiers.

Aquatint. Vignette. 7¾″ by 3¼″. Colored by hand. Undated. Second state, omitting original copyright data of entry by A. Bowen on November 25, 1815.

Stauffer 2909. Grolier 193. Olds 350.

Plate 108 *The Hornet and the Penguin*

Plate 109 *Bainbridge's Squadron Returning from the Mediterranean*

No. 174

Triumphant return of the American Squadron under Com. Bainbridge from the Mediterranean 1815.

M. Corne del. W.S. Leney Sc.

Printed by Saml. Maverick N.Y.

Line engraving. Vignette. 7⅝″ by 3¾″. Colored by hand. Undated. Stauffer 1881. Grolier 194. Olds 352a.

MISCELLANEOUS SAILING WARSHIPS

Plate 110 No. 175

View of the Line of Battle — Ship Pennsylvania The Largest Vessel in the World.

Designed and lithographed expressly for the Philada. Saturday Chronicle, by A. Hoffy, artist & Lithogr. No. 44, Chestnut St. Phila.

DESCRIPTION. This splendid ship was launched in Philadelphia, July 18th. 1837.—Her length from figure-head to stern gallery is 247 ft. 6 inchs.—extreme breadth of beam, 58 ft. 1 1/2 inchs—weight of sheet anchor 11696 lbs.—height from step of mainmast to tip of flypole 278 ft.—canvass for suit of sails 18,344 yards,—number of Guns (32 pounders) 140. Tonnage 3307—Full manned the Ship requires 2000 men.

Designed & drawn on Stone by A. Hoffy. The Ship from a sketch by C.C. Barton, U.S.N.

Lithograph. 18½″ by 14⅜″. Black and white. Rare.

No. 176

U.S. Ship of the Line Pennsylvania, 140 Guns

Lith & Pub by N. Currier. 152 Nassau St. Cor of Spruce N.Y.

Entered according to Act of Congress in the year 1846 by N. Currier, in the clerk's office of the District Court of the Southern District of N.Y.

Tonnage 3000—Length from Figurehead to Stern Gallery 247 ft.—Extreme breadth 85 ft.—Height from bottom of Keel to top of rail amidships 54 ft. Total height from water line to main truck 239 ft. Draught of water 25 ft.

Lithograph. 12¾″ by 8¾″. Colored.

Plate 110 *The Battleship Pennsylvania*

Plate 111 *The USS Delaware*

No. 177

Old Ironsides

HBM Ship Cyane

HBM Ship Levant

WAK Martin Pinx. Copyright 1911 by Harry A. Martin, Ambler, Pa.

No. 65 of 150 proofs printed in colors in facsimile of the original.

Details of each vessel at the sides under each hull.
Lithograph. Colored by hand. The original painting in water color is also in the writer's collection.

No. 178

U.S. Ship Independence

Razee, bearing the broad pennant of Com. Charles Stewart, struck by a Squall, off the coast of America. Sept. 8th. 1842.

Lith. of E.C. Kellogg, 87 Fulton St. N. York 73 Main St. Hartford, Conn.

Drawn by George Filley, one of the crew.

Lithograph. 12¼″ by 8″. Color. Undated.

Plate 111

No. 179

The United States Ship DELAWARE, Captain Henry E. BALLARD, near the Western Islands August 25th. 1833 on her passage to France with his Excellency Edward LIVINGSTON, Envoy Extraordinary and minister Plenipotentiary from the United States to the Court of St. Cloud.

Drawn and Dedicated to his Commander and Mess Mates by their obedient servant F.W. Moores (Sailing Master.)

Print par Antoine Roux (père) à Marseille Lith. de Lemercier

Lith. par Frederic Roux à Paris

Lithograph. 22⅞″ by 15⅜″. Colored by hand. Rare.

Plate 112

No. 180

Old Ironsides On a Lee Shore. The U.S. Frigate Constitution Captn. Elliott, weathering Scilly, on her return from France, with the Hon. Edward Livingston on board the night of the Eleventh of May 1835.

Plate 112 *Old Ironsides on a Lee Shore*

Plate 113 *American Squadron at Sea*

Illustration of a sketch, in the Democratic Review, of April 1839, by the author of "The log of Old Ironsides".

Drawn on Stone by A. Hoffy, from a painting by J. Evans,

P.S. Duval, Lith. Philada.

Entered according to Act of Congress in the year 1839 by Dow and Duval in the clerk's office in the District Court of the Eastern District of Penna.

Published by Dow & Duval.

Lithograph. 23" by 16¼". Colored.

Extremely rare. Not in any known collection. Kennedy Galleries has seen only two copies. This one comes from the Henry Graves collection and was acquired by William M. Ellis of New Orleans. He was interested in the connection of Edward Livingston with Louisiana. While Livingston was certainly an important figure, there is no question in the writer's mind that the inspiration for this lithograph was the fame of the old ship herself.

Plate 113 No. 181

American Squadron at Sea

At top:

No. 1. Pennsylvania—No. 2. Franklin.—No. 3. North Carolina.—No. 4. Scyanne.—No. 5. The Warren.—No. 6. Small Vessels in Company.

Designed and Painted by Robert Walker. On Stone by A. Hoffy, and M. O'Connor.

Entered according to Act of Congress in the Year 1839 by Walker and Duval in the Clerk's Office of the District Court of the Eastern District of Pa.

P.S. Duval Lith Phila.

Published by Walker & Duval, No. 7 Bank Alley Phila.

Lithograph. 25¼" by 17". Colored by hand.

No. 182

Plate 114 *To the Officers, Seamen, and Marines of the U.S. Navy, this view of the Delaware, 74, secured in the Dry-dock. U.S. Navy Yard Gosport, is Dedicated with Great Respect, By their Very Obedient Servant Joseph Goldsborough Bruff.*

Plate 114 *USS Delaware in Dry Dock*

Plate 115 *The Opening of the Dry Dock at Gosport*

Drawn on stone from a Sketch by J.G. Bruff.

Childs and Inman's Lith. Philadelphia

Lithograph. 15½″ by 11⅛″. Colored by hand. First of a pair.

Plate 115 No. 183

This View of the Opening of the Dry Dock U.S. Navy Yard Gosport, is Very Respectfully Dedicated to LOAMMI BALDWIN ESQ.

By his very Obedient Servant, Joseph Goldsborough Bruff.

Drawn on Stone by G.Lehman from a Sketch by J.G. Bruff.

Childs and Inman's Lith. Philadelphia

Lithograph. 15⅜″ by 10½″. Colored by hand. Second of a pair.

* * *

The writer was fortunate to obtain certain rare prints in the latter part of 1973. Two of them illustrate the naval bombardment of Breed's Hill, otherwise known as the Battle of Bunker Hill. Both of these prints were done in Philadelphia in 1775 and are in remarkably good condition. They are certainly among the very earliest engravings done in America. The third is of a privateer action in 1804. The fourth is a watercolor painting of the United States Frigate *Decatur.* Then there is a very rare engraving of the *Chesapeake-Shannon* engagement. Kennedy Galleries know of only three copies extant. Finally, there is the very rare *View of the Bombardment of Fort McHenry,* the occasion on which Francis Scott Key wrote "The Star-Spangled Banner."

Plate 116 No. 184

An Exact View of The Late Battle at Charlestown June 17th, 1775.

In which an advanced party of about 700 Provincials stood an Attack made by 11 Regiments & a Train of Artillery & after an Engagement of two hours Retreated to their Main body at Cambridg Leaving Eleven Hundred of the enemy Killed and Wounded upon the field

REFERENCES

1	*Boston*	4	*Provincial Brestwork*	7	*Somerset*
2	*Charlestown*	5	*Retreating Regulars*	8	*Broken Officer*
3	*Breed's Hill*	6	*Frigate*	9	*General Putnam*

B: Romans in Ære incidit

Plate 116 *An Exact View of the Late Battle at Charlestown*

Plate 117 *A View of the Bombardment of Fort McHenry*

Line engraving. 16⅜" by 11⅛". 1775. Black and white. Engraved by Bernard Romans in Philadelphia. Mentioned in the *Pennsylvania Gazette,* 20 September, 1775.

Stauffer 2731. Stokes & Haskell 1775-B-91. Not in Olds or Grolier. Extremely rare. Other imps.: New-York Historical Society, New York Public Library, Yale University, Metropolitan Museum of Art, Massachusetts Historical Society, John Carter Brown Library.

This print shows two British frigates firing salvos at Breed's Hill. One frigate, HMS *Somerset,* is now lying in the mud off Provincetown, Massachusetts.

No. 185

A Correct View of The Late Battle at Charlestown June 17th, 1775

Aitken Sculp for the Pena. Magae.

Line engraving. Black and white. 9¾" by 7¼". Undated. Published by the *Pennsylvania Gazette,* 20 September, 1775.

Very rare. Stauffer 3. Not in Olds or Grolier. Other imps.: American Antiquarian Society, Worcester; Brown University; Massachusetts Historical Society; Metropolitan Museum of Art; New York Public Library; Wadsworth Atheneum.

No. 186

The Cambrian of Boston, Willm. Marshall Master beating off a French Cutter Privateer, on 23 October 1804

Josh. Cartwright del. 1804 W. Barnard, Engraver.

Boston, Published by C. Cave Feby. 12, 1805.

Aquatint. 16⅝" by 12¾". Colored by hand.

Grolier 198. Olds 539. Rare.

No. 187

The United States Sloop of War Decatur

Watercolor. Artist unknown.

No. 188

The Brilliant Achievement of the Shannon Frigate, Captn. Broke in boarding and capturing the United States Frigate, Chesapeake off Boston, June 1st. 1813 in Fifteen Minutes. Shannon 38 Guns, 330 Men Chesapeake 49 Guns, 440 Men.

Painted & Engraved by W. Elmes. Augt. 1813

Pub[d.] by W[m] Elmes—107 Tottenham Court Road London.

Aquatint. 19¼″ by 14¼″. Colored by hand.

Extremely rare. Not in Olds. Grolier 99.

Plate 117 No. 189

A View of the Bombardment of Fort McHenry, near Baltimore, by the British fleet, taken from the Observatory, under the Command of Admirals Cochrane, & Cockburn, on the morning of the 13[th.] of Sep[r.] 1814, which lasted 24 hours, & thrown from 1500 to 1800 shells, in the Night attempted to land by forcing a passage up the ferry branch but were repulsed with great loss.

Table of references appears at right.

J. Bower sc Phil[a.] Copy Right Secured.

Aquatint. 17⅛″ by 11″. Colored by hand. Undated, circa 1815.

Rare. Olds 318. Grolier 171. Stauffer 236.

Other imps.: Chicago Historical Society, Maryland Historical Society, New-York Historical Society, Peale Museum, Yale University.

* * *

EPILOGUE

Both the collection and accompanying description terminate with the onset of steam. Fulton had built the *Clermont* in 1807, and the first steam warship, USS *Fulton,* was launched in 1815. She was a paddle wheeler, as were several of the warships as late as 1847 at Vera Cruz in the Mexican War. When Ericson invented the screw-driven steamship in 1837, the cumbersome side-wheelers became obsolete, but old salts in the Navy Department were slow to change. Nearly all the warships in the Civil War were sailing auxiliaries, many of them conversions from pure sail.

Duties of the Navy after the War of 1812 evolved into action against piracy and normal peacetime protection of citizens and commerce. This era had its moments of excitement, but it could not be compared with the earlier war period, in terms of either glory or significance.

The War of 1812 was the apogee of the sailing Navy. From an American standpoint, it was far more significant than its place in textbooks would imply. Even Treasury Secretary Gallatin, never one to champion the Navy, declared that this war solidified the States and their independence. It also created national pride and international stature. Granting all that, it is interesting to look at the war through the eyes of a British historian. One is almost amused at the totally different attitude. The Americans are regarded as boastful miscreants, not without justification in many cases.

Britain, it should be recalled, was at war with other nations on a global scale during both conflicts with the United States, whereas the latter with short lines of supply had only to defend two coasts and the northern border. Then, too, the British were fighting against their own kind. Many American officers and men had been trained in the Royal Navy or by others who had served the King. Even the skill of American designers and shipwrights was inherited or imported from Great Britain. In any event, it was not a band of "rag tags" that challenged Britannia, at least not in the War of 1812.

In both wars, the Revolution and the War of 1812, another key factor in American success was the degree of sympathy that many of the enemy held for the colonists. The Howe brothers, Lord Richard and Sir William, commanders respectively of the Navy and Army on the North American station during the early part of the Revolution, were known to share warm feelings toward the rebels. Their older brother George Augustus had fought and been killed at Ticonderoga in the French and Indian War, and the people of Boston honored him by placing a statue in Westminster Abbey.

Sir William's dalliances while in command of the Army at Philadelphia were common knowledge, and his social circle was not limited to Tories or sympathizers with George III. Moreover, the political profile of the anti-war Whigs in Britain was not much lower than it was in the colonies. Thus the ties, political, social, and cultural, must have mitigated the effectiveness with which some of the English leaders prosecuted the war. For example, Admiral Lord Richard Howe was a friend of Benjamin Franklin, and some historians think his goal was to sign a treaty of peace rather than win it in battle. Futhermore, the Howes were not unique. After his disastrous defeat at Saratoga, General John Burgoyne returned to England as an exchanged prisoner on parole. While in this status he took a seat in Parliament and became an outspoken opponent of the war. Dissenters have rarely been popularized but to ignore their impact is to distort the truth.

By the time of 1812, it was again an English trait to look upon Americans and colonists as "bloody colonials." Some statesmen, like Lord Castlereagh, did not share this view, but in Parliament they were the exception. At the professional level, among officers and men of the Royal Navy and British Army, there was wide recognition of American bravery and skill. Many acts of humanity on the part of American officers had won the respect of the enemy. This was particularly apparent in the homage paid to Commodore Perry at the time of his death in Trinidad in 1819. The British garrison had arranged a welcoming ceremony for Perry, who had treated their regiment magnanimously after his victory at Lake Erie. Perry was stricken with fever at sea and died just as his ship was arriving from Venezuela. He was then buried at Trinidad with full military honours and with the governor general in attendance.

The period between the War of 1812 and the War Between the States was transitional, not only from sail to steam but from engraving to lithography. The latter medium was dominated by Nathaniel Currier and his successor, the firm of Currier and Ives. Clipper ships and whaling vessels then captured the public fancy at least as much as did war events. Marine artists here and abroad were no less active, but their subjects had changed. Most important, after the War of 1812 the independence of the United States was never again at issue.

BIOGRAPHICAL SKETCHES OF ARTISTS AND ENGRAVERS

Bailey, John (1750-1819)—An English engraver who did many of the scenes for J. Jenkins' *Naval Achievements of Great Britain* and Gold's *The Naval Chronicle.*

Barralet, John James (1747-1815)—A Philadelphia artist and engraver, born in Ireland of French parents. He came to Philadelphia in 1795 and worked in water colors. He also produced both stipple and line engraving and at one time was in partnership with Alexander Lawson. He died in 1815.

Baugean, Jean Jerome (1764-1819)—A painter and engraver born in Marseilles. Worked in Italy, Marseilles, and Paris. His main reputation was that of a line engraver in Paris.

Birch, Thomas (1779-1851)—Born in London. Settled in the U.S. in 1793 in Philadelphia. First painted portraits, then turned to landscapes and marine paintings, of which his best known were *The United States and Macedonian* and *The Constitution and Guerriere.*

Birch, William Russell (1755-1834)—Born in 1755 at Warwickshire, England. Emigrated to Philadelphia in 1794. Did miniature paintings and many line engravings. Best known for his views of Philadelphia. Father of Thomas Birch.

Bowen, Abel (1790-1850)—A prolific engraver on wood, born in New York State. He published his prints and a number of books in Boston from 1811 to 1836. In 1816, he published *The Naval Monument,* which included both wood and copper engravings, mostly his own. He is especially remembered for his mixed method engraving of the USS *Constitution.* Bowen died in Boston in 1850.

Bower, John—A map engraver who worked in Philadelphia between 1809 and 1819. His work was fairly crude by the standards of the day. Most notable of his work was a primitive type engraving of the bombardment of Fort McHenry in the War of 1812.

Boydell, John—Born in Shropshire in 1719. Died in London in 1804 at the age of 86. He was a very famous engraver and most prolific, having produced 4,432 separate plates during his long career. His achievements as a citizen were so great that he was elected Lord Mayor of London in 1791.

Brooks, John—A specialist in mezzotint said to have been born in Ireland. Went from Dublin to London in 1727. Died about 1760.

Bruff, Joseph Goldsborough (1804-1889)—A topographical draughtsman and artist of Washington, D.C. A graduate of West Point, he did not follow a military career but went into government service.

Cartwright, Joseph—An English marine painter who exhibited subjects at the Royal Academy from 1824 to 1829. He was appointed marine painter to the Admiralty in 1828. Died in 1829.

Chappel, Alonzo (1828-1887)—A painter of portraits, landscapes, and historical subjects, born in New York City. He lived in Brooklyn from 1848 to 1868.

Charles, William (1776-1820)—A Scottish engraver in line, stipple, and aquatint, who hastily departed from Edinburgh because of his caricatures of the dignitaries of that city. He emigrated to New York in 1801 and then in 1814 to Philadelphia. He is best known for his caricatures of events, especially political, surrounding the War of 1812.

Childs, Cephas G. (1793-1871)—A Philadelphia engraver for almost thirty years. He was first involved in Childs and Carpenter. Later the firm was called Childs and Gimber. Still later he associated himself with the artist Henry Inman. The firm was then called Childs and Inman. In 1845 Childs quit the engraving business to become a newspaper editor.

Collet, John (1725-1780)—An English artist, born in London in 1725. Studied under Lambert, the landscape painter. He painted subjects of humor somewhat after the manner of Hogarth. Died in 1780.

Coqueret, Pierre Charles—A French engraver, born in Paris in 1761.

Cornè, Michel Felice (1752-1845)—Born on Elba, Cornè was a successful marine artist who worked in Boston, Salem, and Newport. He was a prolific painter. Many of his works hang in the Peabody Museum at Salem. Many of Abel Bowen's woodcuts were done from Cornè's paintings.

Currier, Nathaniel (1813-1888)—Perhaps the most successful publisher of prints in history. This American, who first practised lithography in Philadelphia with M.E.D. Brown, started his business in New York at the age of twenty-two in 1835. In 1857, Currier took in James Merritt Ives as a partner. The firm preempted the field of timely illustration. No other name even approached them in national standing and commercial success. Currier retired in 1880, and the firm carried on to 1907, when its assets were sold at auction.

Debucourt, Philibert Louis (1755-1832)—A French painter and engraver born in Paris in 1755. His early works were in mezzotint; then he turned to aquatint, for which he was best known. He died at Belleville in 1832.

Dodd, Robert (1748-1816)—An English marine painter active in the latter part of the eighteenth century and early nineteenth century. He concentrated on actions of the Royal Navy and storms at sea. His work was recognized by the Royal Academy.

Doolittle, Amos (1754-1832)—An early line engraver of New Haven, Connecticut, born in 1754 in Cheshire, Connecticut. His training in engraving and silversmithing was under the aegis of Eliakim Hitchcock of Cheshire. He served in the Revolutionary Army at Cambridge and later published line engravings of the battles of Lexington and Concord. His work was primitive in quality, its main virtue today being that it is early and scarce. He died in New Haven in 1832.

Dubourg, M.—A painter and engraver in London in the early nineteenth century. Exhibited several portrait miniatures at the Royal Academy. The Victoria and Albert Museum has some of his aquatints.

Edwin, David (1776-1841)—An engraver in stipple who worked in Philadelphia from 1797 to 1830. He was born in Bath, England, in 1776 and died in Philadelphia in 1841. He was especially noted for portrait engraving, having been trained in this art by a Dutch engraver in London. In Philadelphia, he was first employed by the book publisher T. B. Freeman and later by Edward Savage.

Elliott, William—An officer of the Royal Navy who also happened to be a painter. It was not unusual to have people aboard ship who could sketch and paint. When a lieutenant in 1776, he sketched the action off the Mud Fort of the Delaware. Between 1780 and 1790, he gained some reputation and even exhibited at the Royal Academy in 1789, featuring a painting of the *Bon Homme Richard - Serapis* engagement.

Elmes, William—An English painter and engraver in London in the late eighteenth century. Exhibited at the Royal Academy in 1797.

Fittler, James—An English engraver who combined stipple and line engraving. He studied at the Royal Academy and became an engraver in 1800.

Freeman, T. W.—A print publisher in Philadelphia who in 1813 was in business with J. Pierie.

Garneray, Ambroise Louis (1783-1857)—A French marine painter born in

Paris in 1783. Studied under his father, Jean Francois Garneray. At the age of thirteen, he went to sea and in 1806 he was taken prisoner by the British. He returned to France in 1814 and was patronized by the King. His seascapes and naval actions drew wide attention. In 1833 he was appointed director of the museum at Rouen. Also, he studied aquatint, and designed and engraved sixty-four views of the ports of France and forty views of foreign ports. His works have hung in the following museums: Boulogne, Marseilles, Nantes, Rochefort, Rochelle, Rouen, and Versailles. He died in Paris in 1857.

Gimbrede, Thomas (1781-1832)—A stipple engraver, born in France in 1781. He came to New York in 1802 and painted miniatures. His major effort, however, was devoted to the engraving of portraits, mostly of the heroes of the day. In 1819, he was appointed drawing master at West Point, where he remained until his death in 1832.

Haghe, Louis—An early master of lithography, born in Belgium in 1806. He gained a reputation at an early age in his native country, but at some point he moved to London. He is famous for his brilliant lithographs of the *Chesapeake-Shannon* engagement, which, being one of the few British victories in the War of 1812, helped achieve instant popularity for these plates.

Haid, Johann Philip—An engraver, son of Johann Lorenz Haid, born at Augsburg in 1730. He died in 1806.

Hassell, J.—An English draughtsman and engraver who did aquatints in the late eighteenth and early nineteenth century.

Havell, Robert—An English printmaker specializing in aquatint in the early 1800's. His son, Robert Havell, Jr., came to New York in 1840 and gained fame for his plates for Audubon's *Birds of America.*

Heath, James A. E. (1757-1834)—An English engraver who apprenticed under Collyer. He was an associate engraver of the Royal Academy and was named engraver to the King in 1794.

Hill, John (1770-1850)—Born in London, he trained as an engraver and did a number of views after Turner. In 1816, he came to Philadelphia and then moved to New York.

Hoffy, A.—An American lithographer born in England about 1790. Was working on stone in New York in 1835. He moved to Philadelphia in 1838, and from 1839 to 1841 he produced illustrations for *U.S. Military Magazine,* published by Huddy and Duval. He continued his work in Philadelphia until 1860.

Hoogland, William—An American engraver in line and stipple who worked in New York around 1815. Later he worked with Abel Bowen in Boston.

Huggins, William John (1781-1845)—An English marine painter, born in 1781. Went to sea in early life with the merchant marine. He had exhibits at the Royal Academy, and in 1834 he was appointed marine painter to William IV. Three of his scenes of Trafalgar hang at Hampton Court Palace. His death occurred in 1845.

Jarvis, John Wesley (1780-1840)—Born in England, came to Philadelphia at the age of five. He apprenticed under Edward Savage in Philadelphia and afterwards moved to New York. He attained fame as a portrait painter of the American school.

Jazet, Jean Pierre Marie—A French engraver, born in Paris in 1788. Studied under his uncle Debucourt, who was well known for aquatints. He died in 1871.

Kearney, Francis—A famed American engraver in line, stipple, and then aquatint. He was born in Perth Amboy, New Jersey, about 1780. From 1810 to 1833 he engaged in the engraving business in Philadelphia.

Kensett, Thomas—An American engraver, born in England in 1786. He was a member of the firm of Shelton and Kensett of Cheshire, Connecticut. He was best known for his maps. His death occurred in 1829.

Kimberly, Denison—Born in Guilford, Connecticut, in 1814. He learned line engraving under Asoph Willard in Hartford. In 1830, he was working in Boston but by 1858 he had abandoned engraving and was painting portraits in Hartford.

Kneass, William—An American line engraver born in Lancaster, Pennsylvania, in 1781. He worked in Philadelphia from 1805 to 1840, the year of his death.

Kobell, Hendrik—A Dutch marine painter, born in Rotterdam in 1751. He was first known for sketches and drawings and then executed works in oil. The Amsterdam Academy accepted him after his return from England. Later he moved to Rotterdam, where he painted naval engagements. He died there in 1782.

Lawson, Alexander—An American engraver on copper, born in Scotland in 1773, died in Philadelphia in 1846. He first worked for Thackara and Vallance in Philadelphia but then went into business for himself.

While military or naval actions were not his usual subject, his engraving of *Perry's Victory* after Birch was and is a famous work.

Longacre, James B. (1794-1869)—A Philadelphia portrait engraver who learned his profession under George Murray. From 1844 until his death he was engraver to the U.S. Mint.

Martin, William A. K. (1817-1867)—A Philadelphia marine painter who worked in water colors. His detail drawings of early nineteenth century American warships show expert knowledge of ships and rigging.

Maverick, Peter (1780-1831)—Born in New York, son of an early engraver. He worked on copper and later added lithography.

Montardier—A French marine water colorist whose first name is unknown. He worked in Havre during the 1820's and early 1830's. The Peabody Museum has nine of his paintings.

Murray, George—Born in Scotland. Came to Philadelphia about 1800, where he engaged in portrait engraving. He founded the engraving firm of Murray, Draper, Fairman & Co. He died in 1822.

Notté, Claude Jacques—A French portrait and miniature painter, born at Montreuil-sur-Marne. Exhibited at the Salon de Correspondance from 1779 to 1795. One of his subjects was the celebrated John Paul Jones.

Owen, James (1824-1877)—A lithographer in Philadelphia. Studied under Wagner and McGuigan and did many works for P.S. Duval, publisher of *U.S. Military Magazine.*

Paton, Richard—An English marine painter born in 1717. In early life he was taken to sea by Admiral Sir Charles Knowles. It is uncertain where or how he acquired the art of painting but at middle age his paintings became popular and he exhibited at the Society of Arts and the Royal Academy. He died at the age of 74 in 1791.

Peale, Rembrándt—Son of Charles Willson Peale, born in Bucks County, Pennsylvania, in 1778. He painted portraits of many eminent Americans of the day, including President Thomas Jefferson, Mrs. James Madison, Commodore Bainbridge, Commodore Perry, and Commodore Decatur. He established himself as a portrait painter in Charleston, South Carolina, around 1796. Then he studied under West in London, after which he returned to Philadelphia in 1809. Peale died in 1860.

Peltro, John—An English engraver of the late eighteenth century who did work in the marine field but was better known for topographical prints.

Perrot, Ferdinand Victor—A French painter born in Paimboeuf in 1808. He executed a large number of lithographs, for which he is best known. He died in Russia, succumbing to the climate, in 1841.

Pocock, Nicholas—A very prolific and famous English marine painter born at Bristol in 1741. Early in his life he commanded a merchant vessel. Starting with sketches, he came to the notice of Sir Joshua Reynolds. His first exhibit at the Royal Academy was in 1782. His specialty was naval battles. He was one of the founders of the Water Colour Society in Britain. Died at Maidenhead, 1821.

Rawdon, Ralph—An American engraver associated with Thomas Kensett in Cheshire, Connecticut, around the time of the War of 1812. In 1816 he moved to Albany, where he conducted a general engraving business.

Reinagle, Hugh (1790-1834)—A well-known American painter who studied under John Holland. He worked in both oils and water colors and did city views as well as historical scenes.

Rosenberg, Christian—An English printmaker specializing in aquatint in the early 1800's.

Savage, Edward—An American engraver born in Princeton, Massachusetts, 1761. Died there in 1817. Originally a goldsmith, he turned to painting and then to stipple and mezzotint engraving. He studied in London where he learned the art of engraving, but in 1794 he returned to the States and settled in Philadelphia. He did the first known aquatints in America—the two *Constellation-L'Insurgente* prints in 1799.

Schetky, John Christian—A marine water colorist born in Edinburgh in 1778. He enjoyed a distinguished career first as a professor of civil drawing at both Military and Naval Academies and then as marine painter to the Duke of Clarence, George IV, William IV, and Queen Victoria, in succession. He died in London in 1874.

Serres, Dominic—Born in France in 1722. Went to sea in a merchant vessel and was captured by the English in 1752. Became a marine painter and later a member of the Royal Academy. He was appointed marine painter to George III. Died in 1793.

Seymour, Samuel—An American engraver located in Philadelphia 1797-1822. He engraved portraits and city views, as well as naval engagements. He disappeared on a Western exploration in 1823.

Steel, James W. (1799-1879)—A Philadelphian who apprenticed in the engraving business under Benjamin Tanner. He became established as a line engraver but turned in his later years to bank note engraving.

Strickland, William—An American engraver and architect born in Philadelphia in 1787. After first taking up portrait painting he turned to engraving and finally to architecture. He is best known for his views of the War of 1812.

Stuart, Gilbert—Born in Rhode Island in 1754. Went to England and trained under Benjamin West. Achieved acclaim as a portraitist. Returned to America in 1793 and resided chiefly in Philadelphia and Washington. In 1805, he moved to Boston, where he died in 1828. His more famous paintings included several of George Washington, Sir Joshua Reynolds, Benjamin West, and many lesser known figures of the day in Britain and America.

Sully, Thomas—A famous American portrait painter, born in England in 1783. At the age of nine he went to America with his parents, who were actors. Later he returned to England to study under West. In 1838, he settled in Philadelphia, where he died in 1872.

Sutherland, Thomas—An American engraver born in New York, 1775. In 1805, he moved to Philadelphia where he did both line and stipple engraving. His greatest achievements seem to have the War of 1812 as their core subject. He carried on the engraving business and map and print publishing until 1845. He died in Baltimore in 1848.

Tiebout, Cornelius—One of the best known engravers of the early nineteenth century in Philadelphia. He was born in New York in 1777 of Dutch Huguenots whose family had come to this country as early as 1656. In 1793, he went to London to study the art of engraving. He reached his peak during the War of 1812. He died in Kentucky in or around 1830.

Walters, Samuel (1811-1882)—Born at sea, son of Miles Walters, a ship painter. Became a marine painter in Liverpool. Then in 1845 he moved to London, but in 1847 he returned to Liverpool, where he exhibited a series of Dutch scenes. The Peabody Museum has twelve paintings by or attributed to him.

Whitcombe, Thomas—An English marine painter, born around 1760. His work centered around storms at sea and naval battles. His paintings were exhibited at the Royal Academy from 1703 to 1824.

Wright, John—A miniature painter who practiced in London in the early part of the 1800's. His work was exhibited at the Royal Academy between 1795 and 1819. He committed suicide in 1820.

BIBLIOGRAPHY

Allen, Gardner W. *A Naval History of the American Revolution.* Boston and New York: Houghton Mifflin & Co., 1913.

Anonymous. *Sketches of Naval Life with Notices of Men, Manners and Scenery on the Shores of the Mediterranean.* Ezekiel Howe, Publisher, 1829.

Badger, Barber. *The Naval Temple.* Boston: Barber Badger, Publisher, 1816.

Baker, William A. *Colonial Vessels—Some Seventeenth Century Sailing Craft.* Barre, Mass.: Barre Publishing Co., 1962.

Bowen, A. *The Naval Monument.* Boston: George Clark, 1830.

Brenton, Edward Pelham. *The Naval History of Great Britain from the Year 1783 to 1822.* London: J. F. Dove, 1823.

Bryan. *Bryan's Dictionary of Painters and Engravers.* London: G. Bell & Sons Ltd., 1918.

Burgess, Fred. *Old Prints and Engravings.* New York: Tudor Publishing Co., 1937.

Chapelle, Howard. *The History of the American Sailing Navy: The Ships and Their Development.* New York: Bonanza Books, 1949.

Clark, William Bell. *George Washington's Navy.* Baton Rouge, Louisiana: Louisiana State University Press, 1960.

__________. *Naval Documents of the American Revolution.* Washington: Navy Department, 1964.

Clement, Clara Erskine. *Painters, Sculptors, Architects and Engravers.* Boston and New York: Houghton Mifflin, 1893.

Clement & Hutton. *Artists of the Nineteenth Century.* Boston and New York: Houghton Mifflin & Co., 1893.

Clowes, William Laird. *The Royal Navy—A History from the Earliest Times to the Present.* London: Sampson Low, Marston & Co., Ltd., 1897.

Cooper, J. Fenimore. *The History of the Navy of the United States of America.* Paris: W. Galignaur & Co., Inc., 1839.

Drepperd, Carl W. *Early American Prints.* New York and London: The Century Co., 1930.

Fielding, Mantle. *American Engravers upon Copper and Steel.* Philadelphia, 1917.

Fiske, John. *The American Revolution.* Boston: Houghton Mifflin & Co., 1896.

Fletcher, James, and Rivington, James. *The Naval History of Great Britain with the Lives of the most illustrious Admirals and Commanders, from the Reign of Queen Elizabeth.* London, 1758.

Griffin, Martin I. J. *Commodore John Barry.* Published by the author. Philadelphia, 1903.

The Grolier Club. *The United States Navy 1776 to 1815.* New York, 1942.

Grove, George C., and Wallace, David A. *The New-York Historical Society's Dictionary of Artists in America.* New Haven: Yale University Press, 1957.

Guthridge, Leonard F., and Smith, Jay D. *The Commodores.* New York: Harper and Row, 1969.

Hagerman, John F., and Woodward, Major E. M. *History of Burlington and Mercer Counties, New Jersey.* Philadelphia: Press of J. B. Lippincott & Co., 1883.

Haskell, Daniel C, and Stokes, I. N. Phelps. *American Historical Prints—Early Views of American Cities, etc.* New York: New York Public Library, 1933.

Janes, William. *Military Occurrences of the Late War between Great Britain and the United States of America.* London: Black, Kingsbury, Parbury, and Allen, 1818.

Kay, James, Jr., & Brother. *History of the Late War.* Pittsburgh: H. M. Brackenridge, 1846.

Kennedy Galleries, Inc. *Notable American Prints: The Collection of Henry Graves, Jr.* New York, 1959.

Letter from the Secretary of State to Mr. Monroe on the Subject of the Attack on the Chesapeake; The Correspondence of Mr. Monroe with the British Government; and also Mr. Madison's Correspondence with Mr. Rose, on the same Subject. March 23, 1808. Printed by Order of the House of Representatives. Washington: A. & G. Way, Printers.

Lossing, Benson J. *Pictorial Field Book — War of 1812.* New York: Harper & Bros., 1818.

Maclay, Edgar Stanton. *History of the Navy.* New York: Appleton's, 1895.

Mahan, Alfred Thayer. *Major Operations of the Navy in the War of American Independence.* Boston: Little, Brown & Co., 1913.

Mahan, Capt. Alfred Thayer. *Sea Power in its Relations to the War of 1812.* Boston: Little ,Brown & Co., 1905.

The Museum of Graphic Art. *American Printmaking — The First 150 Years.* New York: Museum of Graphic Arts. Designed and printed by Chanticleer Press, 1969.

Navy Department. *American Naval Fighting Ships.* Washington, 1959.

Neeser, Robert Wilden. *Statistical and Chronological History of the United States Navy 1775-1907.* The Macmillan Co., 1909.

Olds, Irving S. *Bits and Pieces of American History.* New York, 1952.

The Peabody Museum of Salem. *Catalogue of a Special Exhibition of the Irving S. Olds Collection of American Naval Prints and Paintings.* Salem, 1959.

Peters, Harry T. *Currier & Ives, Printmakers to the American People.* New York: Doubleday Doran, 1942.

Philadelphia Directories 1812-1815.

Redgrave, Samuel. *A Dictionary of Artists of the English School.* London: George Bell and Sons.

Robinson, Charles N. *Old Naval Prints—Their Artists and Engravers.* London: The Studio Limited, 1924.

Robison, S. S. *A History of Naval Tactics from 1530 to 1930.* Annapolis: U. S. Naval Institute, 1942.

Roosevelt, Theodore. *The Naval War of 1812.* Published privately.

Shippen, Edward. *Naval Battles Ancient and Modern.* Philadelphia: J. C. McCurdy & Co., 1883.

Slater, J. Herbert. *Engravings and Their Value.* London: L. Upcott Gill, 1900.

Spears, John R. *The History of Our Navy.* New York: Charles Scribner, 1899.

Stauffer, David McNeely. *American Engravers upon Copper and Steel.* New York: The Grolier Club, 1907.

Stevens, William Oliver & Westcott, Allan. *A History of Sea Power.* New York: Doubleday Doran, 1920.

U. S. Government Printing Office. *Naval Documents related to the Quasi War between the United States and France.* Washington, 1936.

U. S. Government Printing Office. *Naval Documents related to the United States Wars with the Barbary Powers.* Washington, 1937.

Wainwright, Nicholas B. *Commodore James Biddle and his Sketch Book.* Philadelphia: The Historical Society of Pennsylvania, 1966.